Norton Anthology of Western Music
In Two Volumes

Volume I

Medieval • Renaissance • Baroque

Also available from Norton

Choral Music: A Norton Historical Anthology
  Edited by Ray Robinson

The Norton Scores: An Anthology for Listening
  Third Edition: Standard and Expanded
  Edited by Roger Kamien

The Concerto, 1800–1900
  Edited by Paul Henry Lang

The Symphony, 1800–1900
  Edited by Paul Henry Lang

An Anthology of Early Renaissance Music
  Edited by Noah Greenberg and Paul Maynard

The Solo Song, 1580–1730
  Edited by Carol MacClintock

NORTON ANTHOLOGY OF WESTERN MUSIC

In two volumes

VOLUME I

Medieval · Renaissance · Baroque

Edited by Claude V. Palisca

YALE UNIVERSITY

W · W · NORTON & COMPANY

NEW YORK · LONDON

First Edition

Library of Congress Cataloging in Publication Data
Main entry under title:
Norton anthology of western music.
  Includes indexes.
  CONTENTS: v. 1. Medieval, Renaissance, baroque.—
v. 2. Classic, romantic, modern.
  1. Vocal music. 2. Instrumental music. I. Palisca,
Claude V.
M1N825 [M1495] [M5] 780.8'2   80–11916
ISBN 0–393–95143–X (v. 1)
ISBN 0–393–95151–0 (v. 2)
1 2 3 4 5 6 7 8 9 0

To J., C., and M.

Contents

RENAISSANCE

MOTET

MASS

CHANSON, LIED, CANTO CARNASCIALESCO

Preface

The title of this anthology lacks one important qualifier: it is a *historical* anthology of western music. There is a wide difference between a historical anthology and one intended simply to supply a selection of music for study and analysis.

A historian cannot confine himself to studying the great works in splendid isolation that are the usual stuff of anthologies. He is interested in products of the imagination great and small as they exist in a continuum of such works. Just as composers did not create in a musical void, standing aloof from the models of their predecessors and contemporaries, so the historically-oriented student and analyst must have the primary material that permits establishing historical connections. This anthology invites students and teachers to make such connections. It confronts, for example, important works and their models, pieces written on a common subject or built according to similar procedures or that give evidence of subtle influences of one composer's work on another's.

Most music before 1500 was composed on some pre-existent music, and there are numerous examples of this practice even after that date. Whenever possible in this anthology, the music that served to ignite a composer's imagination is provided. In one notable case a single chant gave rise to a chain of polyphonic elaborations. This is the Alleluia with verse, *Alleluia Pascha nostrum* (NAWM 13), elaborated by Leonin in organum purum with clausulae, refreshed with substitute clausulae by his successors; and both his and the new clausulae were turned into motets by adapting Latin or French texts to them or made fuller with new parts both with and without texts. (This Alleluia set, although different in content, format and realization, is itself modeled on similar sets on this chant devised by Richard Crocker and Karl Kroeger as local teaching aids, and I am indebted to them for the general idea and certain details).

A similar chain of works are the masses built upon the melisma on the word *caput* in the Sarum version of the Antiphon, *Venit ad Petrum:* three are here given, the first possibly by Dufay, the second by Obrecht, and the third by Ockeghem, each in turn influencing the next (NAWM 35, 36, and 37). It is instructive similarly to observe in Josquin's early motet, *Tu solus, qui facis mirabilia* (NAWM 29), the way he absorbed fragments of Ockeghem's arrangement of the song, *D'ung aultre amer* (NAWM 44), or to be able to refer to the *Benedictus* of Taverner's Mass, *Gloria tibi trinitas* (NAWM 38), the source of the famous subject, *In nomine,* when studying one of the many varia-

tions upon it, that by Christopher Tye (NAWM 61). The process of coloration and variation that produced Luys de Narváez's arrangement for vihuela (NAWM 45b) may be
inferred from comparing it to the original polyphonic chanson *Mille regretz* by Josquin
(NAWM 45a). A later example of this process, starting with a monodic model, may be
found in the *Lachrimae* pavans of Dowland, Byrd, Farnaby, and Sweelinck (NAWM
98a, b, c, and d) based on the well-known air, *Flow my tears,* by Dowland (NAWM
66). In the twentieth century the variation procedure is the structural principle for several excerpts, namely those by Strauss (NAWM 142), Schoenberg (NAWM 145), and
Copland (NAWM 147). Arcadelt's parody in his Mass (NAWM 39) of Mouton's
motet, *Noe, noe* (NAWM 31) may be assumed to be a tribute, but what of Handel's
similar recycling of Urio's *Te Deum* (NAWM 86) in *Saul* (NAWM 87)?

More subtle connections may be detected between Lully's overture to *Armide*
(No. 73a) and the opening chorus of Bach's cantata, *Nun komm, der Heiden Heiland*
(NAWM 88), between Gossec's *Marche lugubre* (NAWM 113) and the Funeral March
from Beethoven's "Eroica" Symphony (NAWM 114), between the nocturnes of Field
and Chopin (NAWM 121 and 122), or between Mussorgsky's song *Les jours de fête*
(NAWM 154) and Debussy's *Nuages* (NAWM 140).

Comparison of the musical realization of the same dramatic moments in the
legend of Orpheus by Peri and Monteverdi (NAWM 68 and 69) reveal the latter's debts
to the former. Again, two orchestral commentaries on the Queen Mab speech in *Romeo
and Juliet* highlight the distinct gifts of Berlioz (NAWM 125) and Mendelssohn
(NAWM 126) as tone poets. It is revealing to compare the settings of Mignon's song
from Goethe's *Wilhelm Meister* by Schubert, Schumann and Wolf (NAWM 129, 130,
and 131), or Grandi and Schütz in their respective versions of a text from the *Songs of
Songs* (NAWM 82 and 84).

Some of the selections betray foreign influences, as the penetration of Italian
styles in England in Purcell's songs for *The Fairy Queen* (NAWM 74) or Humfrey's
verse and anthem (NAWM 85). The crisis in Handel's career, brought on partly by the
popularity of the ballad opera and the English audience's rejection of his own Italian
opera seria, is documented in a scene from *The Beggar's Opera* (NAWM 78) and by
the changes within his own dramatic *oeuvre* (NAWM 77, 79 and 87). The new Italian
style to which he also reacted is exemplified by Pergolesi's felicitous cantata on the
Orpheus myth (NAWM 117).

Some composers are represented by more than one work to permit comparison of
early and late styles—Josquin, Monteverdi, Bach, Handel, Vivaldi, Haydn, Beethoven, Liszt, Schoenberg, Stravinsky—or to show diverse approaches by a single composer to distinct genres—Machaut, Dufay, Ockeghem, Arcadelt, Willaert, Monteverdi, Bach, Mozart.

A number of the pieces marked new departures in their day, for example Adrian
Willaert's *Aspro core* from his *Musica nova* (NAWM 52), Nicola Vicentino's chro-
matic *Laura che'l verde lauro* (NAWM 54), Viadana's solo concerto, *O Domine Jesu
Christe* (NAWM 81), Rousseau's scene from *Le devin du village* (NAWM 118), or C.
P. E. Bach's sonata (NAWM 104). Other pieces were chosen particularly because they
were singled out by contemporary critics, such as Arcadelt's *Ahime, dov'è 'l bel viso*
(NAWM 51), hailed in 1549 by Bishop Cirillo Franco as a ray of hope for the future of

text-expressive music; or Monteverdi's *Cruda Amarilli* (NAWM 64), dismembered by Artusi in his dialogue of 1600 that is at once a critique and a defense of Monteverdi's innovations; Caccini's *Perfidissimo volto* (NAWM 63), mentioned in the preface to his own *Euridice* as one of his pioneering attempts, or Cesti's *Intorno all'idol mio* (NAWM 72), one of the most cited arias of the mid-seventeenth century. Others are Lully's monologue in *Armide, Enfin il est en ma puissance* (NAWM 73b), which was roundly criticized by Rousseau and carefully analyzed by Rameau and d'Alembert; the scene of Carissimi's *Jephte* (NAWM 83), singled out by Athanasius Kircher as a triumph of the powers of musical expression; and the *Danse des Adolescentes* in Stravinsky's *Le Sacre* (NAWM 143), the object of a critical uproar after its premiere.

Certain of the items serve to correct commonplace misconceptions about the history of music. Cavalieri's *Dalle più alte sfere* (NAWM 67) of 1589 shows that florid monody existed well before 1600. The movements from Clementi's and Dussek's sonatas (NAWM 105 and 106) reveal an intense romanticism and an exploitation of the piano that surpass Beethoven's writing of the same period and probably influenced it. The movement from Richter's String Quartet (NAWM 107) tends to refute Haydn's paternity of the genre. Sammartini's and Stamitz's symphonic movements (NAWM 109 and 110) show that there was more than one path to the Viennese symphony. The Allegro from Johann Christian Bach's E-flat Harpsichord Concerto (NAWM 115) testifies to Mozart's dependence on this earlier model (NAWM 116). The scene from Meyerbeer's *Les Huguenots* (NAWM 135) is another seminal work that left a trail of imitations.

Most of the selections, however, are free of any insinuations on the part of this editor. They are simply typical, superlative creations that represent their makers, genres, or times outstandingly. Most of the *Ars nova* and many of the Renaissance works are in this category, as are a majority of those of the Baroque, Romantic, and Modern periods. My choices mark important turning points and shifts of style, historical phenomena that are interesting if not always productive of great music, new models of constructive procedures, typical moments in the work of individual composers, and always challenging exemplars for historical and structural analysis.

The proportion of space assigned to a composer or work is not a reflection of my estimation of his greatness, and, regretfully, numerous major figures could not be represented at all. In an anthology of limited size every work chosen excludes another of corresponding size that is equally worthy. Didactic functionality, historical illumination, intrinsic musical quality rather than "greatness" or "genius" were the major criteria for selection.

The inclusion of a complete Office (NAWM 2) and a nearly complete Mass (NAWM 1) deserves special comment. I realize that the rituals as represented here have little validity as historical documents of the Middle Ages. It would have been more authentic, perhaps, to present a mass and office as practiced in a particular place at a particular moment, say in the twelfth century. Since the Vatican Council, the liturgies printed here are themselves archaic formulas, but that fact strengthens the case for their inclusion, for opportunities to experience a Vespers service or Mass sung in Latin in their classic formulations are rare indeed. I decided to reproduce the editions of the modern chant books, with their stylized neumatic notation, despite the fact that they are not *urtexts*, because these books are the only resources many students will have available for this repertory, and it should be part of their training to become familiar with the editorial conventions of the Solesmes editions.

These volumes of music do not contain any commentaries, because only an extended essay would have done justice to each of the selections. By leaving interpretation to students and teachers, I hope to enrich their opportunities for research and analysis, for discovery and appreciation. Another reason for not accompanying the music with critical and analytical notes is that this anthology was conceived as a companion to Donald J. Grout's *A History of Western Music,* as revised with my participation in this classic text's Third Edition. Brief discussions of almost every number in this collection will be found in that book: some barely scratch the surface, others are extended analytical and historical reflections. An index to these discussions by number in this anthology is at the back of each volume.

The anthology, it must be emphasized, was intended to stand by itself as a selection of music representing every important trend, genre, national school and historical development or innovation.

The translations of the poetic and prose texts are my own except where acknowledged. They are literal to a fault, corresponding to the original line by line, if not word for word, with consequent inevitable damage to the English style. I felt that the musical analyst prefers precise detail concerning the text that the composer had before him rather than imaginative and evocative writing. I am indebted to Ann Walters for helping with some stubborn medieval Latin poems and to Ingeborg Glier for casting light on what seemed to me some impenetrable lines of middle-high German.

A number of research assistants, all at one time students at Yale, shared in the background research, in many of the routine tasks, as well as in some of the joys of discovery and critical selection. Robert Ford and Carolyn Abbate explored options in pre-Baroque and post-Classical music respectively during the selection phase. Gail Hilson and Kenneth Suzuki surveyed the literature on a sizeable number of the items, while Susan Cox Carlson contributed her expertise in early polyphony. Clara Marvin assisted in manifold ways in the last stages of this compilation.

My colleagues at Yale were generous with their advice on selections, particularly Elizabeth Keitel on Machaut, Craig Wright on Dufay, Leon Plantinga on Clementi, John Kirkpatrick on Ives, and Allen Forte on Schoenberg. Leeman Perkins' and Edward Roesner's suggestions after seeing preliminary drafts of the Medieval and Renaissance sections contributed to rounding out those repertories. I am also indebted to Paul Henry Lang for his reactions to the classic period choices and to Christoph Wolff for those of the Baroque period.

The Yale Music Library was the indispensable base of operations, and its staff a prime resource for the development of this anthology. I wish to thank particularly Harold Samuel, Music Librarian, and his associates Alfred B. Kuhn, Kathleen J. Moretto, Karl W. Schrom, Kathryn R. Mansi, and Warren E. Call for their many favors to me and my assistants.

Most of all I have to thank Claire Brook, whose idea it was to compile an anthology to accompany the Third Edition of *A History of Western Music.* Her foresight, intuition, and creative editorial style gave me confidence that somehow within a short space of time this complex enterprise would unfold. Thanks to the quotidian efforts of her assistant, Elizabeth Davis, who with remarkable efficiency and insight steered the project through a maze of production pitfalls, we were able to achieve the goal of bringing out the anthology and text together.

Professor Grout's text set a standard of quality and scope that was my constant challenge and inspiration. For his enthusiastic acceptance of the project, his cooperation, and his willingness to subordinate proprietary and justly prideful feelings to a pedagogical ideal of historical text-*cum*-anthology, the users of these tools and I owe a great debt, particularly if this coupling achieves a measure of the success that his book has enjoyed.

W. W. Norton and I are grateful to the individuals and publishers cited in the footnotes for permission to reprint, re-edit or adapt material under copyright. Where no modern publication is cited, the music was edited from original sources.

Finally, to my wife Jane, and my son and daughter, Carl and Madeline, to whom this anthology is dedicated with affection, I must express my gratitude for patiently enduring the deprivations, hibernations, even estivations, over the years of gestation required by this and the companion work.

Claude V. Palisca
Branford, Connecticut

Instructions for reading modern plainchant notation.

One line of the four-line staff is designated by a clef as either middle C (♭) or the F immediately below it (♭). These are not absolute but relative pitches. The *neumes,* as the shapes are called, are usually assigned equal durations, although at one time they may have had some temporal significance. Two or more neumes in succession on the same line or space, if on the same syllable, are sung as though tied. Composite neumes, representing two or more pitches, are read from left to right, except for the *podatus* or *pes* (♭), in which the lower note is sung first. Oblique neumes (◣) stand for two different pitches. A neume, whether simple or composite, never carries more than one syllable. Flat signs, except in a signature at the beginning of a line, are valid only until the next vertical division line or until the beginning of the next word.

The Vatican editions, such as the *Liber Usualis* (*LU*), employ, in addition a number of interpretive signs, based on the performance practices of the Benedictine monks of the Solesmes Congregation. A horizontal dash above or below a neume means it is to be slightly lengthened. A vertical stroke above or below a note marks the beginning of a rhythmic unit when this would not otherwise be obvious. A dot after a note doubles its value. Vertical bars of varied lengths show the division of a melody into periods (full bar), phrases (half-bar), and smaller members (a stroke through the uppermost staff-line). The note-like symbol on a space or line at the end of the staff is a *custos* (guard), a guide to lead the reader to the first note on the following line.

An asterisk in the text shows where the chorus takes over from the soloist, and the signs *ij* and *iij* (ditto and double–ditto) indicate that the preceding phrase is to be sung twice or three times.

a) *Introit*

Ordinaries from Mass XI, *LU*, pp. 46–48; propers from *LU*, 497–501.

vit de témplo sáncto sú- o vó- cem mé- am.

Ps. Dí-ligam te Dómine, forti-túdo mé- a : * Dóminus firma-

méntum mé-um, et re-fúgi-um mé-um, et liberá-tor mé-us.

Gló-ri- a Pátri.   E u o u a e.

Repeat Introit, *Circumdederunt me . . . vocem meam.*

b) Kyrie

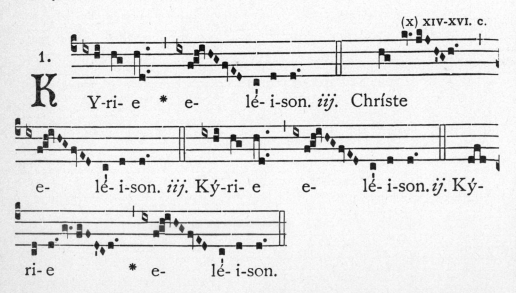

(x) XIV-XVI. C.

1.

K Y-ri- e * e- lé- i-son. *iij.* Chríste

e- lé- i-son. *iij.* Ký-ri- e e- lé- i-son. *ij.* Ký-

ri- e * e- lé- i-son.

(The *Gloria in excelsis* is not sung from Septuagesima Sunday until Easter, except on Maundy Thursday, Holy Saturday, and Feast days).

c) *Collect*

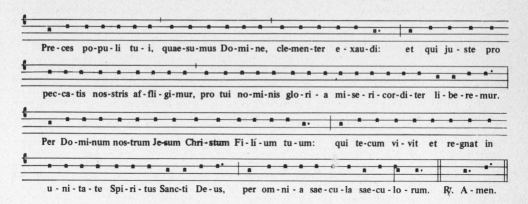

Pre - ces po-pu-li tu - i, quae-su-mus Do-mi-ne, cle-men-ter e - xau-di: et qui ju - ste pro

pec-ca-tis nos-stris af - fli - gi-mur, pro tui no-mi-nis glo-ri - a mi-se-ri-cor-di-ter li-be-re-mur.

Per Do-mi-num nos-trum Je-sum Chri-stum Fi - lí - um tu - um: qui te-cum vi-vit et re-gnat in

u - ni - ta - te Spi-ri-tus Sanc-ti De-us,   per om-ni-a sae-cu-la sae-cu-lo-rum. ℟. A-men.

d) *Epistle*

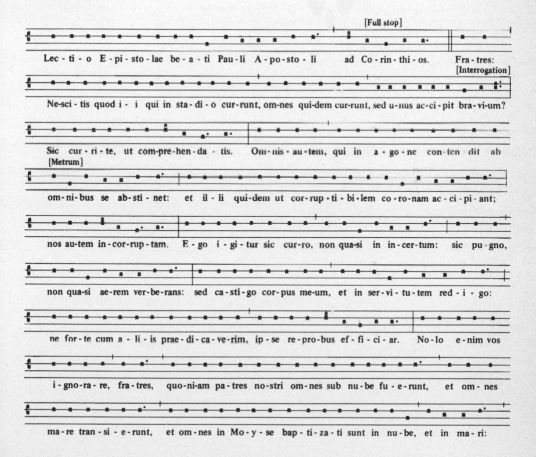

[Full stop]

Lec-ti-o E-pi-sto-lae be-a-ti Pau-li A-po-sto-li   ad Co-rin-thi-os.   Fra-tres:

[Interrogation]

Ne-sci-tis quod i - i qui in sta-di-o cur-runt, om-nes qui-dem cur-runt, sed u-nus ac-ci-pit bra-vi-um?

Sic cur - ri - te, ut com-pre-hen-da - tis.   Om-nis-au-tem, qui in a - go-ne con-ten dit ab
[Metrum]

om-ni-bus se ab-sti-net: et il-li qui-dem ut cor-rup-ti-bi-lem co-ro-nam ac-ci-pi-ant;

nos au-tem in-cor-rup-tam. E - go i - gi-tur sic cur-ro, non qua-si in in-cer-tum: sic pu-gno,

non qua-si ae-rem ver-be-rans: sed ca-sti-go cor-pus me-um, et in ser-vi-tu-tem red-i-go:

ne for-te cum a - li - is prae-di-ca-ve-rim, ip-se re-pro-bus ef-fi-ci-ar.   No-lo e-nim vos

i - gno-ra-re, fra-tres, quo-ni-am pa-tres no-stri om-nes sub nu-be fu-e-runt,   et om-nes

ma-re tran-si-e-runt, et om-nes in Mo-y-se bap-ti-za-ti sunt in nu-be, et in ma-ri:

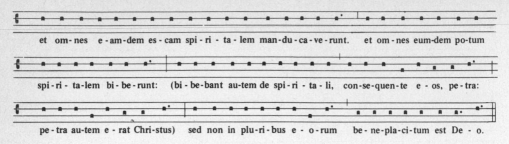

et om-nes e-am-dem es-cam spi-ri-ta-lem man-du-ca-ve-runt.   et-nes eum-dem po-tum

spi-ri-ta-lem bi-be-runt: (bi-be-bant au-tem de spi-ri-ta-li, con-se-quen-te e-os, pe-tra:

pe-tra au-tem e-rat Chri-stus)   sed non in plu-ri-bus e-o-rum   be-ne-pla-ci-tum est De-o.

e) *Gradual*

Grad. 3.

A Djú-   tor * in opportu-ni-   tá- ti- bus,

in tri-bu-la-ti-ó-   ne : spé-rent in   te,

qui nové-runt te :   quó-ni-am non   dere-

línquis quae-réntes te,   Dó-   mi- ne.

℣. Quó-ni-am non

in fí-nem oblí-vi-o   é-rit páupe-ris :

pa-ti-énti-a páu- pe- rum non per-í-bit in ae-tér-

num : exsúrge, Dómi- ne,· non praevá- le-

at * hó- mo.

f) *Tract*

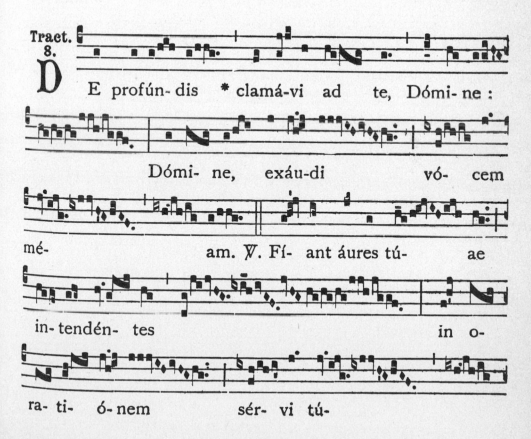

E profún-dis * clamá-vi ad te, Dómi-ne :

Dómi- ne, exáu-di vó- cem

mé- am. ℣. Fí- ant áures tú- ae

in-tendén- tes in o-

ra- ti- ó-nem sér- vi tú-

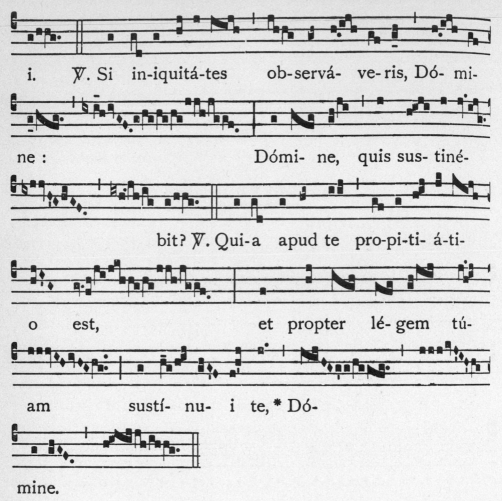

i. ℣. Si in-iquitá-tes   ob-servá- ve- ris, Dó- mi-

ne :   Dómi- ne, quis sus- tiné-

bit? ℣. Qui-a   apud te pro-pi-ti- á-ti-

o   est,   et propter lé- gem tú-

am   sustí- nu- i te,* Dó-

mine.

g) *Gospel*

Do-mi-nus vo-bis-cum. ℟. Et cum spi-ri-tu tu-o.   Se-quen-ti-a san-cti E-van-ge-li-i

se-cun-dum Mat-thae-um. ℟. Glo-ri-a ti-bi Do-mi-ne.   In il-lo tem-po-re:

Di-xit Je-sus di-sci-pu-lis su-is pa-ra-bo-lam hanc: Si-mi-le est re-gnum

cae - lo-rum ho - mi - ni   pa - tri - fa - mi - li - as,   qui e - xi - it pri-mo ma - ne con -du - ce - re

[Conclusion]

o - pe-ra-ri - o in vi-ne-am su - am ... Mul-ti e-nim sunt vo-ca - ti,   pau-ci ve - ro e - lec - ti.

h) Credo

XI. c.

4.

CRédo   in únum Dé-um, Pátrem omnipot-éntem, fa-

ctórem caéli   et térrae, vi-si-bí-li-um ómni- um,   et invi-

si-bí-li- um. Et in únum Dóminum Jésum Chrístum, Fí-

li- um Dé- i unigéni- tum.   Et ex Pátre nátum   ante

ómni- a saécu- la. Dé-um de Dé- o, lúmen de lúmine,

Dé-um vérum de Dé-o véro. Géni-tum, non fáctum, consub-

stanti-á-lem Pátri : per quem ómni- a fácta sunt. Qui pro-

pter nos hómines,   et propter nóstram sa-lú-tem descéndit

de caé-lis.   Et incarná-tus est de Spí-ri-tu Sáncto   ex

Ma-rí- a Vírgi-ne :   Et hómo fáctus est. Cru-ci-fíxus ét-i- am

pro nóbis : sub Pónti- o Pi-lá-to   pássus, et sepúltus est.

Et resurréxit térti- a dí- e,   secúndum Scriptúras.   Et

ascéndit in caélum : sédet ad déxte-ram Pátris. Et í-te-rum

ventúrus est cum gló-ri- a,   judi-cá-re vívos et mórtu- os :

cú-jus régni non é-rit fí-nis.   Et in Spí-ri-tum Sánctum, Dó-

minum,   et vi-vi-fi-cántem : qui ex Pátre Fi-li- óque procé-

dit. Qui cum Pátre et Fí-li- o   simul ado-rá-tur,   et con-

glo-ri-fi-cá-tur : qui locútus est per Prophé-tas.   Et únam sán-

ctam cathó-li-cam   et apostó-li-cam Ecclé-si- am.   Confí-

te- or únum baptísma   in remissi- ónem pecca-tó-rum. Et

exspécto resurrecti- ónem mortu-ó-rum. Et ví-tam ventú-

ri sać-cu-li.   A-   men.

i) *Offertory*

Offert.
8.

B Onum est * confi-té- ri Dómi- no,   et

psál-   le- re   nó- mi- ni tú- o,   Al-tíssime.

(Preface omitted)

j) Sanctus

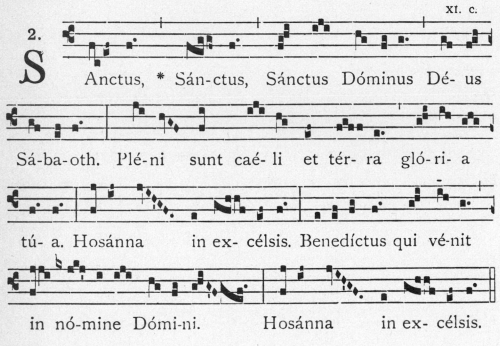

Anctus, * Sán-ctus, Sánctus Dóminus Dé- us Sá-ba-oth. Pléni sunt caé- li et tér- ra gló-ri- a tú- a. Hosánna in ex- célsis. Benedíctus qui vé-nit in nó-mine Dómi-ni. Hosánna in ex- célsis.

(*Pater noster* omitted)

k) Agnus Dei

- gnus Dé- i, *qui tóllis peccá- ta múndi : mi-se-ré-re nóbis. Agnus Dé- i, *qui tól- lis peccá-ta mún-

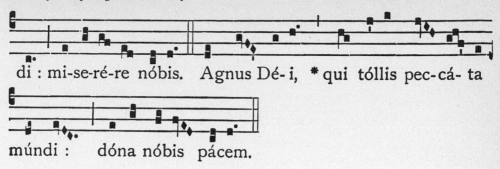

di : mi-se-ré-re nóbis.   Agnus Dé- i,   * qui tóllis pec-cá- ta

múndi :   dóna nóbis pácem.

l) *Communion*

Comm.
1.
I Llú-mi-na * fá-ci-em tú-am super sérvum tú- um,

et sálvum me   fac   in tú-   a mi- se-ri-córdi-   a :

Dó-mine, non confúndar,   quó-ni- am invo- cá- vi   te.

m) Benedicamus Domino

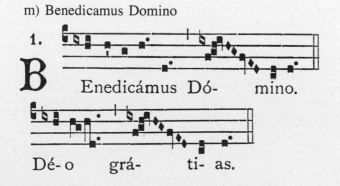

1.
B   Enedicámus Dó-   mino.

Dé- o   grá-   ti- as.

Introit

Ps. 17. 5, 6, 7, 2-3

Circumdederunt me gemitus mortis, dolores inferni circumdederunt me: et in tribulatione mea invocavi Dominum, et exaudivit de templo sancto suo vocem meam. *Ps.* Diligam te, Domine, fortitudo mea: Dominus firmamentum meum, et refugium meum, et liberator meus. ℣. Gloria Patri.

The groans of death surround me, the sorrows of hell encompassed me: and in my affliction I called upon the Lord, and He heard my voice, from His holy temple. *Ps. 17, 2, 3.* I will love Thee, O Lord, my strength: the Lord is my firmament, and my refuge and my deliverer. ℣. Glory.

Kyrie

Kyrie eleison.
Christe eleison.
Kyrie eleison.

Lord have mercy.
Christ have mercy.
Lord have mercy.

Collect

Preces populi tui, quaesumus, Domine, clementer exaudi: ut, qui juste pro peccatis nostris affligimur, pro tui nominis gloria misericorditer liberemur. Per Dominum.

Do Thou, we beseech Thee, O Lord, graciously hear the prayers of Thy people, that we, who are justly afflicted for our sins, may be mercifully delivered for the glory of Thy name. Through our Lord.

Epistle

1 Cor. 9, 24–27; 10, 1–5

Lectio Epistolae beati Pauli Apostoli ad Corinthos.

Fratres: Nescitis quod ii qui in stadio currunt, omnes quidem currunt, sed unus accipit bravium? Sic currite, ut comprehendatis. Omnis autem qui in agone contendit, ab omnibus se abstinet: et illi quidem ut corruptibilem coronam accipiant; nos autem incorruptam. Ego igitur sic curro, non quasi in incertum: sic pugno, non quasi aerem verberans: sed castigo corpus meum, et in servitutem redigo: ne forte cum aliis praedicaverim, ipse reprobus efficiar. Nolo enim vos ignorare, fratres, quoniam patres nostri omnes sub nube fuerunt, et omnes mare transierunt, et omnes in Moyse baptizati sunt in nube, et in mari: et omnes eamdem escam spiritalem manducaverunt, et omnes eumdem potum spiritalem biberunt: (bibebant autem de spiritali, consequente eos, petra: petra autem erat Christus): sed non in pluribus eorum beneplacitum est Deo.

Lesson from the Epistle of blessed Paul the Apostle to the Corinthians.

Brethren, know you not that they that run in the race, all run indeed, but one receiveth the prize? So run, that you may obtain. And every one that striveth for the mastery, refraineth himself from all things: and they indeed that they may receive a corruptible crown, but we an incorruptible one. I therefore so run, not as at an uncertainty; I so fight, not as one beating the air: but I chastise my body, and bring it into subjection: lest perhaps, when I have preached to others, I myself should become a castaway. For I would not have you ignorant, brethren, that our fathers were all under the cloud, and all passed through the sea; and all in Moses were baptized, in the cloud and in the sea; and all did eat the same spiritual food, and all drank the same spiritual drink; (and they drank of the spiritual rock that followed them; and the rock was Christ). But with the most of them God was not well pleased.

Text and translation from F. X. Lasance and F. A. Walsh, *The New Roman Missal.* (New York: Benziger Press, 1950). Reprinted by permission.

Gradual

Ps. 9. 10–11, 19–20

Adjutor in opportunitatibus, in tribulatione: sperent in te, qui noverunt te: quoniam non derelinquis quaerentes te, Domine. ℣. Quoniam non in finem oblivio erit pauperis: patientia pauperum non peribit in aeternum: exsurge, Domine non praevaleat homo.

The helper in due time, in tribulation: let them trust in Thee, who know Thee: for Thou dost not forsake them that seek Thee, O Lord. ℣. For the poor man shall not be forgotten to the end: the patience of the poor shall not perish for ever: arise, O Lord, let not man be strengthened.

Tract

Ps. 129. 1–4

De profundis clamavi ad te, Domine: Domine, exaudi vocem meam. ℣. Fiant aures tuae intendentes in orationem servi tui. ℣. Si iniquitates observaveris, Domine: Domine, quis sustinebit? ℣. Quia apud te propitiatio est, et propter legem tuam sustinui te, Domine.

From the depths I have cried to Thee, O Lord; Lord, hear my voice. ℣. Let Thine ears be attentive to the prayer of Thy servant. ℣. If Thou shalt observe iniquities, O Lord, Lord, Who shall endure it? ℣. For with Thee is propitiation, and by reason of Thy law I have waited for Thee, O Lord.

Gospel

In illo tempore: Dixit Jesus discipulis suis parabolam hanc: Simile est regnum caelorum homini patrifamilias, qui exiit primo mane conducere operarios in vineam suam. Conventione autem facta cum operariis ex denario diurno, misit eos in vineam suam. Et egressus circa horam tertiam, vidit alios stantes in foro otiosos, et dixit illis: Ite et vos in vineam meam, et quod justum fuerit, dabo vobis. Illi autem abierunt. Iterum autem exiit circa sextam et nonam horam: et fecit similiter. Circa undecimam vero exiit, et invenit alios stantes, et dicit illis: Quid hic statis tota die otiosi? Dicunt ei: Quia nemo nos conduxit. Dicit illis: Ite et vos in vineam meam. Cum sero autem factum esset, dicit dominus vineae procuratori suo: Voca operarios, et redde illis mercedem, incipiens a novissimis usque ad primos. Cum venissent ergo qui circa undecimam horam venerant, acceperunt singulos denarios. Venientes autem et primi, arbitrati sunt quod plus essent accepturi: acceperunt autem et ipsi singulos denarios. Et accipientes murmurabant adversus patremfamilias, dicentes: Hi novissimi una hora fecerunt, et pares illos nobis fecisti, qui portavimus pondus diei, et aestus. At ille respondens uni eorum, dixit: Amice,

At that time, Jesus spoke to His disciples this parable: The kingdom of heaven is like to a householder, who went out early in the morning to hire laborers into his vineyard. And having agreed with the laborers for a penny a day, he sent them into his vineyard. And going out about the third hour, he saw others standing in the marketplace idle, and he said to them, Go you also into my vineyard, and I will give you what shall be just: and they went their way. And again he went out about the sixth and the ninth hour, and did in like manner. But about the eleventh hour, he went out, and found others standing; and he saith to them, Why stand you here all the day idle? They say to him, Because no man hath hired us. He saith to them, Go you also into my vineyard. And when evening was come, the lord of the vineyard saith to his steward, Call the laborers, and pay them their hire, beginning from the last even to the first. When therefore they were come that came about the eleventh hour, they received every man a penny. But when the first also came, they thought that they should receive more; and they also received every man a penny. And receiving it, they murmured against the master of the house,

non facio tibi injuriam: nonne ex denario convenisti mecum? Tolle quod tuum est, et vade: volo autem et huic novissimo dare sicut et tibi. Aut non licet mihi quod volo facere? an oculus tuus nequam est, quia ego bonus sum? Sic erunt novissimi primi, et primi novissimi. Multi enim sunt vocati, pauci vero electi.

saying, These last have worked but one hour, and thou hast made them equal to us that have borne the burden of the day and the heat. But he answering, said to one of them, Friend, I do thee no wrong; didst thou not agree with me for a penny? Take what is thine, and go thy way: I will also give to this last even as to thee. Or, is it not lawful for me to do what I will? is thy eye evil, because I am good? So shall the last be first, and the first last. For many are called, but few are chosen.

Credo

Credo in unum Deum, Patrem omnipotentem, factorem caeli et terrae, visibilium omnium et invisibilium.
Et in unum Dominum Jesum Christum Filium Dei unigenitum. Et ex Patre natum ante omnia saecula. Deum de Deo, lumen de lumine, Deum verum de Deo vero. Genitum, non factum, consubstantialem Patri: per quem omnia facta sunt. Qui propter nos homines et propter nostram salutem descendit de caelis. Et incarnatus est de Spiritu Sancto ex Maria Virgine: et homo factus est. Crucifixus etiam pro nobis: sub Pontio Pilato passus, et sepultus est. Et resurrexit tertia die, secundum Scripturas. Et ascendit in caelum sedet ad dexteram Patris. Et iterum venturus est cum gloria judicare vivos et mortuos: cujus regni non erit finis. Et in Spiritum Sanctum, Dominum et vivicantem: qui ex Patre, Filioque procedit. Qui cum Patre, et Filio simul adoratur, et conglorificatur: qui locutus est per Prophetas. Et unam sanctam catholicam et apostolicam Ecclesiam. Confiteor unum baptisma in remissionem peccatorum. Et expecti resurrectionem mortuorum Et vitam venturi saeculi. Amen.

I believe in one God, Father almighty, maker of heaven and earth and of all things visible and invisible. And in one Lord Jesus Christ, the only-begotten Son of God, born of the Father before all ages. God of God, light of light, true God of true God. Begotten, not made, being of one substance with the Father, by whom all things were made. Who for us men and for our salvation came down from heaven. And was made incarnate by the Holy Ghost of the Virgin Mary, and was made man. And was crucified for us under Pontius Pilate. He suffered and was buried. And the third day he rose again according to the Scriptures. And ascended into heaven, and sitteth on the right hand of the Father. And he shall come again with glory to judge the quick and the dead; of whose kingdom there shall be no end. And in the Holy Ghost, Lord and giver of life, who proceedeth from the Father and the Son. Who, together with the Father and the Son, is worshiped and glorified; who spake by the prophets. And one holy, Catholic, and Apostolic Church. I acknowledge one baptism for the remission of sins. And I look for the resurrection of the dead, and the life of the world to come. Amen.

Offertory

Ps. 91, 2
Bonum est confiteri Domino, et psallere nomini tuo, Altissime.

It is good to give praise to the Lord, and to sing to Thy name, O Most High.

Sanctus

Sanctus, Sanctus, Sanctus Dominus Deus Sabaoth. Pleni sunt caeli et terra gloria tua. Hosanna in excelsis. Benedictus qui venit in nomine Domini. Hosanna in excelsis. [Canon] Per omnia saecula saeculorum. R Amen.

Holy, holy, holy, Lord God of Hosts. The heavens and earth are full of thy glory. Hosanna in the highest. Blessed is he who comes in the name of the Lord. Hosanna in the highest. [Canon] World without end, Rx Amen.

Agnus Dei

Agnus Dei, qui tollis peccata mundi: miserere nobis. Agnus Dei, qui tollis peccata mundi: miserere nobis. Agnus Dei, qui tollis peccata mundi: dona nobis pacem.

Lamb of God, who takest away the sins of the world, have mercy on us. Lamb of God, who takest away the sins of the world, have mercy on us. Lamb of God, who takest away the sins of the world, give us peace.

Communion

Ps. 30. 17–18

Illumina faciem tuam super servum tuum, et salvum me fac in tua misericordia: Domine, non confundar, quoniam invocavi te.

Make Thy face to shine upon Thy servant, and save me in Thy mercy. Let me not be confounded, O Lord, for I have called upon Thee.

Benedicamus Domino

Benedicamus Domino.
Deo gratias.

Let us bless the Lord.
Thanks be to God.

a) *Verse,* Deus in adjutorium

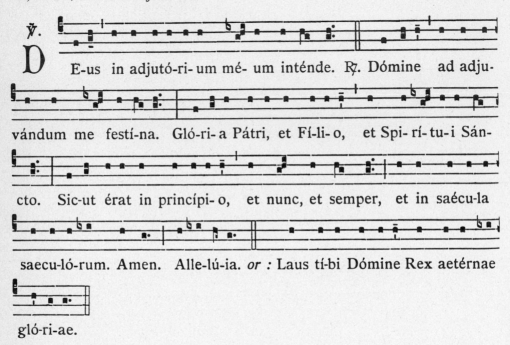

℣. D E-us in adjutó-ri- um mé- um inténde. ℟. Dómine ad adju-

vándum me festí-na. Gló-ri- a Pátri, et Fí-li- o, et Spi- rí- tu- i Sán-

cto. Sic-ut érat in princípi- o, et nunc, et semper, et in saécu-la

saecu-ló-rum. Amen. Alle-lú-ia. *or :* Laus tí-bi Dómine Rex aetérnae

gló-ri-ae.

b) *Antiphon,* Tecum principium

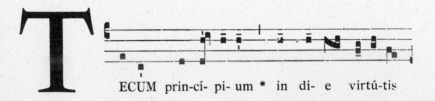

T ECUM prin-cí- pi- um * in di- e virtú-tis

The Chapter, *Kyrie, Pater noster,* and Prayer (*Oratio*) have been omitted. Antiphons, Short Responsory and Verse *Notum fecit* from *AM,* pp. 245–49. *Deus in adjutorium: LU,* p. 112; Psalm 109: *LU,* p. 128, Tone lg; Psalm 110: *LU,* p. 132, Tone 7a; Psalm 111: *LU,* p. 146, Tone 7d; Psalm 129: *LU,* p. 130, Tone 4a; *Magnificat: LU,* p. 213, Tone 1g².

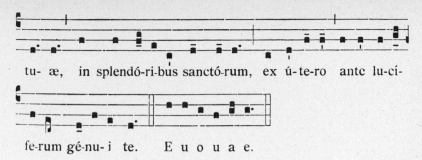

tu- æ,   in splendó-ri-bus sanctó-rum,   ex ú-te-ro   ante lu-cí-

fe-rum gé-nu- i te.   E u o u a e.

c) *Psalm 109,* Dixit Dominus

A model for realizing the psalm formula is given for Psalm 110.

Mediant of 2 accents.   **g**

1. Dí-xit Dóminus Dómino mé-   o ; * Séde a *déxtris* mé-   is.

2. Donec pónam inimicos túos, * scabéllum pé*dum tu*órum.
3. Vírgam virtútis túae emíttet Dóminus ex Sion : * domináre in médio inimic*órum tu*órum.
4. Técum princípium in díe virtútis túae in splendóribus sanctó-rum : * ex útero ante luciferum *gén*ui te.
5. Jurávit Dóminus, et non paenitébit éum : * Tu es sacérdos in aetérnum secúndum órdi*nem Mel*chisedech. (D² : *Mel*chisedech.)
6. Dóminus a déxtris túis, * confrégit in díe irae *súae* réges.
7. Judicábit in natiónibus, implébit ruinas : * conquassábit cápita in térra mul*tórum.
8. De torrénte in via bibet : * proptérea exalt*ábit* cáput.
9. Glória Pátri, et Fílio, * et Spir*ítui* Sáncto.
10. Sicut érat in princípio, et núne, et sémper, * et in saécula saecu-*lórum.* Amen.

Return to Antiphon, *Tecum principium*

d) *Antiphon,* Redemptionem misit Dominus

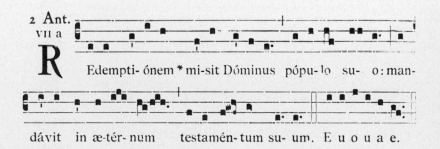

2 Ant.
VII a

R

Edempti- ónem * mi-sit Dóminus pópu-lo   su-   o: man-

dávit in æ-tér- num   testamén-tum su- um. E u o u a e.

e) *Psalm 110,* Confitebor tibi Domine

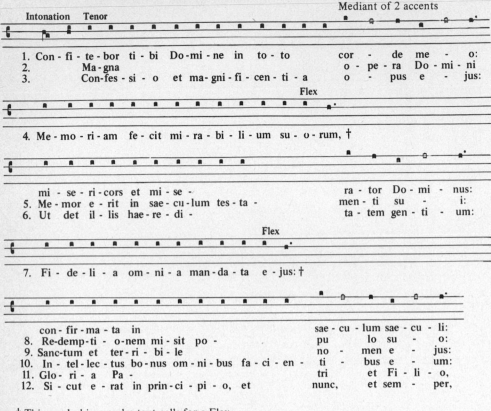

Mediant of 2 accents

Intonation   Tenor

1. Con - fi - te - bor ti - bi Do - mi - ne in to - to   cor - de me - o:
2. Ma - gna   o - pe - ra Do - mi - ni
3. Con - fes - si - o et ma - gni - fi - cen - ti - a   o - pus e - jus:

Flex

4. Me - mo - ri - am fe - cit mi - ra - bi - li - um su - o - rum, †

mi - se - ri - cors et mi - se -   ra - tor Do - mi - nus:
5. Me - mor e - rit in sae - cu - lum tes - ta -   men - ti su - i:
6. Ut det il - lis hae - re - di -   ta - tem gen - ti - um:

Flex

7. Fi - de - li - a om - ni - a man - da - ta e - jus: †

con - fir - ma - ta in   sae - cu - lum sae - cu - li:
8. Re - demp - ti - o - nem mi - sit po -   pu - lo su - o:
9. Sanc - tum et ter - ri - bi - le   no - men e - jus:
10. In - tel - lec - tus bo - nus om - ni - bus fa - ci - en -   ti - bus e - um:
11. Glo - ri - a Pa -   tri et Fi - li - o,
12. Si - cut e - rat in prin - ci - pi - o, et   nunc, et sem - per,

† This symbol in a psalm text calls for a Flex.

* This symbol in a psalm text marks the closing versicle, which is sung to the Tenor followed by the Termination

◘ The hollow note is sung when there are two unaccented syllables after the accented one, as in *ó-pe-ra Dó-mi-ni.*

f) *Antiphon,* Exortum est in tenebris

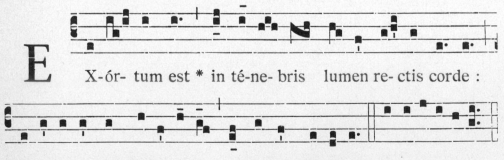

E X - ór - tum est * in té - ne - bris lumen re - ctis corde :

mi - sé - ri - cors et mi - se - rá - tor, et justus Dómi - nus. E u o u a e.

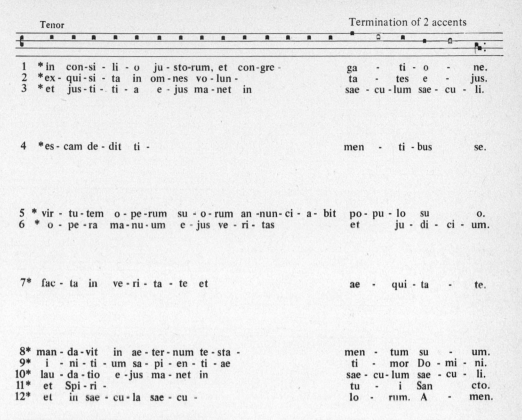

Tenor   Termination of 2 accents

1 *in con-si - li - o   ju - sto-rum, et con-gre -   ga - ti - o - ne.
2 *ex - qui-si - ta in om-nes vo-lun -   ta - tes e - jus.
3 *et jus-ti- ti - a   e - jus ma-net in   sae - cu-lum sae - cu - li.

4 *es- cam de - dit ti -   men - ti - bus   se.

5 * vir - tu-tem o - pe-rum su - o-rum an -nun- ci - a- bit po- pu - lo su   o.
6 * o - pe -ra ma-nu-um e - jus ve - ri - tas   et   ju - di - ci - um.

7* fac - ta in ve - ri - ta - te et   ae - qui - ta - te.

8* man - da -vit in ae - ter - num te - sta -   men - tum su - um.
9* i - ni - ti - um sa - pi - en - ti - ae   ti - mor Do - mi - ni.
10* lau - da - tio e - jus ma - net in   sae - cu- lum sae - cu - li.
11* et Spi - ri -   tu - i San   cto.
12* et in sae - cu - la sae - cu -   lo - rum. A - men.

Return to Antiphon, *Redemptionem*

g) *Psalm 111*, Beatus vir qui timet Dominum

A model for realizing the psalm formula is given for Psalm 110.

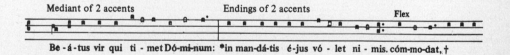

Mediant of 2 accents   Endings of 2 accents   Flex

Be - á -tus vir qui ti - met Dó-mi-num: *in man-dá-tis é-jus vó - let ni - mis. cóm-mo-dat, †

      2. Pótens in térra érit sé*men* éjus : * generátio rectórum be*nedi*cétur.
      3. Glória et divítiae in dómo éjus : * et justítia éjus mánet in saé-*culum* saéculi.
      4. Exórtum est in ténebris lú*men* réctis : * miséricors, et miserá*tor*, *et* jústus.
      5. Jucúndus hómo qui miserétur et cómmodat, † dispónet sermónes súos in *ju*dicio : * quia in aetérnum non commo*vé*bitur.
      6. In memória aetérna é*rit* jústus : * ab auditióne mála *non tí*mébit.
      7. Parátum cor éjus speráre in Dómino, † confirmátum est *cor* éjus : * non commovébitur donec despíciat ini*micos* súos.

8. Dispérsit, dédit paupéribus : † justítia éjus mánet in saéculum saéculi : * córnu éjus exaltábitur in glória.

9. Peccátor vidébit, et irascétur, † déntibus súis frémet et tabéscet : * desidérium peccatórum perìbit.

10. Glória Pátri, et Fílio, * et Spirítui Sáncto.

11. Sicut érat in princípio, et nunc, et sémper, * et in saécula saeculórum. Amen.

Return to Antiphon, *Exortum*

h) *Antiphon,* Apud Dominum

A-pud Dóminum * mi-se- ri- córdi- a,   et co- pi- ó-

sa   apud e- um red-émpti- o.   E u o u a e.

i) *Psalm 129,* De profundis clamavi ad te

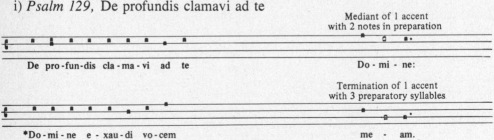

Mediant of 1 accent
with 2 notes in preparation

De pro -fun-dis cla -ma - vi ad te   Do - mi - ne:

Termination of 1 accent
with 3 preparatory syllables

*Do - mi - ne e - xau - di vo -cem   me - am.

2. Fíant áures túae intendéntes * in vócem deprecatiónis méae.

3. Si iniquitátes observáveris Dómine : * Dómine, quis sustinébit?

4. Quia apud te propitiátio est : * et propter légem túam sustínui te Dómine.

5. Sustínuit ánima méa in vérbo éjus : * sperávit ánima méa in Dómino.

6. A custódia matutína usque ad nóctem, * spéret Israel in Dómino.

7. Quia apud Dóminum misericórdia : * et copiósa apud éum redémptio.

8. Et ípse rédimet Israel * ex ómnibus iniquitátibus éjus.

9. Glória Pátri, et Fílio, * et Spirítui Sáncto.

10. Sicut érat in princípio, et nunc, et sémper, * et in saécula saeculórum. Amen.

Return to Antiphon, *Apud Dominum*

j) *Short Responsory,* Verbum caro

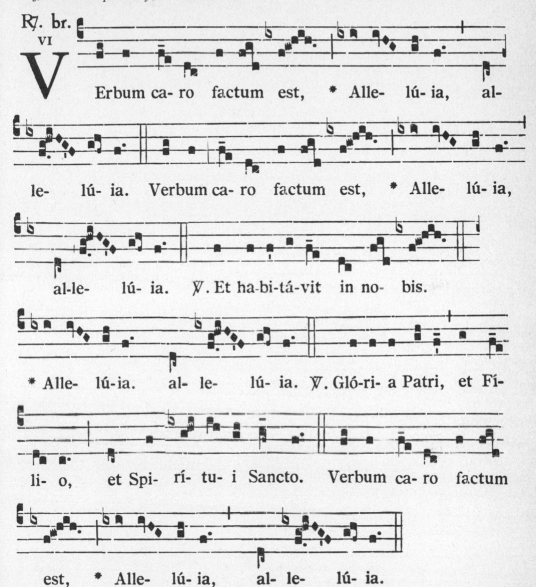

R℣. br.

VI

Verbum ca- ro factum est, * Alle- lú- ia, al-

le- lú- ia. Verbum ca- ro factum est, * Alle- lú- ia,

al-le- lú- ia. ℣. Et ha-bi-tá-vit in no- bis.

* Alle- lú-ia. al- le- lú- ia. ℣. Gló-ri- a Patri, et Fí-

li- o, et Spi- rí- tu- i Sancto. Verbum ca- ro factum

est, * Alle- lú- ia, al- le- lú- ia.

k) *Hymn,* Christe Redemptor omnium

Hriste Red-émptor ómni- um, Ex Patre Patris ú- ni-

ce,   So-lus ante prin-cí-pi- um   Na-tus in-ef-fa- bí- li- ter.

l) *Verse,* Notum fecit

℣. No-tum fe-cit Dómi-nus,   alle- lú-ia.

℟. Sa-lu-tá-re su- um, alle- lú- ia.

m) *Antiphon,* Hodie Christus natus est

Odi- e * Chri- stus na-tus est : hó-di- e Salvá-tor

appá-ru- it : hó-di- e in terra canunt Ange-li, lætán- tur Ar-

chánge- li : hó-di- e   exsúl- tant justi, di-céntes : Gló-ri-   a

in excélsis De- o, alle- lú- ia.   E u o u a e.

n) *Canticle,* Magnificat

Mediant of 1 accent with 3 preparatory syllables (and an extra note in anticipation of the accent in dactylic cadences).

Endings of 1 accent with 2 preparatory syllables.

Tone 1.   g²

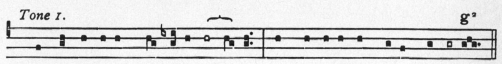

1. Magní- fi-cat *   ánima *mé- a* **Dóminum.**
2. Et exsultávit *spi- ri-tus* **mé**- us * in Dé- o sa-lu- *tá-ri* **mé**-   o.

> 3. Quia respéxit humilitátem *ancillae* súae : * ecce enim ex hoc beá-
> tam me dícent ómnes genera*tió*nes.
> 4. Quia fécit míhi *mágna qui* pótens est : * et sánctum nó*men* éjus.
> 5. Et misericórdia éjus a progénie *in prog*énies * timén*tibus* éum.
> 6. Fécit poténtiam in *bráchio* súo : * dispérsit supérbos ménte cór*dis*
> súi.
> 7. Depósuit po*téntes de* séde, * et exalt*ávit* húmiles.
> 8. Esuriéntes *implévit* bónis : * et dívites dimísit in*ánes.*
> 9. Suscépit Israel *púerum* súum, * recordátus misericórdi*ae* súae.
> 10. Sicut locútus est *ad pátres* nóstros, * Abraham et sémini éjus *in*
> saécula.
> 11. Glória *Pátri, et* Fílio, * et Spirítu*i* Sáncto.
> 12. Sicut érat in princípio, *et nunc, et* sómper, * et in saécula saecu-
> *lórum.* Amen.

Return to Antiphon, *Hodie Christus*

Verse

V. Deus, in adiutorium meum intende.	V. O God, come to my assistance.
R. Domine, ad adiuvandum me festina.	R. O Lord, make haste to help me.
Gloria Patri, et Filio, et Spiritui Sancto. Sicut erat in principio, et nunc, et semper, et in saecula saeculorum. Amen. Alleluia.	Glory be to the Father, and to the Son, and to the Holy Ghost. As it was in the beginning, is now and ever shall be, world without end. Amen. Alleluia.

English translation from *The Saint Andrew Daily Missal,* ed. Dom Gaspar Lefebvre, O.S.B. (New York: Benziger Press, 1956). Reprinted by permission.

Antiphon with Psalm 109

Tecum principium in die virtutis tuae in splendoribus sanctorum, ex utero ante luciferum genui te.

With Thee is the principality in the day of Thy strength in the brightness of the Saints, from the womb before the day star I begot Thee.

Dixit Dominus Domino meo: sede a dextris meis: Donec ponam inimicos tuos scabellum pedum tuorum.
Virgam virtutis tuae emittet Dominus ex Sion: dominare in medio inimicorum tuorum.

The Lord said unto my Lord: Sit Thou at My right hand. Until I make Thine enemies Thy footstool.
The Lord shall send the rod of Thy strength out of Sion: rule Thou in the midst of Thine enemies.

Tecum principium in die virtutis tuae in splendoribus sanctorum: ex utero ante luciferum genui te.

Thine shall be the dominion in the day of Thy power, amid the brightness of the saints: from the womb, before the day star have I begotten Thee.

Iuravit, Dominus, et non poenitebit eum: Tu es sacerdos in aeternum secundum ordinem Melchisedech.
Dominus a dextris tuis, confregit in die irae suae reges.
Iudicabit in nationibus, implebit ruinas: conquassabit capita in terra multorum.

The Lord hath sworn, and will not repent: Thou art a Priest for ever after the order of Melchisedech.
The Lord at Thy right hand shall strike through kings in the day of His wrath.
He shall judge among the heathen, He shall fill the places with dead bodies: He shall wound the heads over many countries.

De torrente in via bibet: propterea exaltabit caput.
Gloria Patri, et Filio, et Spiritui Sancto.

He shall drink of the brook in the way: therefore shall he lift up his head.
Glory be to the Father, and to the Son, and to the Holy Ghost.

Sicut erat in principio, et nunc, et semper, et in saecula saeculorum. Amen.

As it was in the beginning, is now, and ever shall be, world without end. Amen.

Antiphon with Psalm 110

Redemptionem misit Dominus populo suo, mandavit in aeternum testamentum suum.

The Lord hath sent redemption to His people, He hath commanded His convenant for ever.

Confitebor tibi, Domine, in toto corde meo: in consilio iustorum, et congregatione.

I will praise Thee, O Lord, with my whole heart: in the assembly of the upright, and in the congregation.

Magna opera Domini: exquisita in omnes voluntates eius.
Confessio et magnificentia opus eius: et iustitia eius manet in saeculum saeculi.
Memoriam fecit mirabilium suorum, misericors et miserator Dominus: escam dedit timentibus se.

The works of the Lord are great, meet to serve for the doing of His will.
His work is honourable and glorious, and His righteousness endureth for ever.
He hath made a memorial of His wonderful works: the Lord is gracious and full of compassion. He hath given meat unto them that fear Him:

Memor erit in saeculum testamenti sui: virtutem operum suorum annuntiabit populo suo:

He will ever be mindful of His convenant. He will show His people the power of His works;

Ut det illis haereditatem gentium: opera manuum eius veritas et iudicium.

That He may give them the heritage of the heathen. The works of His hands are verity and judgment:

Fidelia omnia mandata eius: confirmata in saeculum saeculi: facta in veritate et aequitate.

All His commandments are sure; they stand fast for ever and ever, being done in truth and uprightness.

Redemptionem misit populo suo: mandavit in aeternum testamentum suum.

He sent redemption unto His people: He hath commanded His covenant for ever:

Sanctum et terribile nomen eius: initium sapientiae timor Domini.

Holy and terrible is His name. The fear of the Lord is the beginning of wisdom:

Intellectus bonus omnibus facientibus eum: laudatio eius manet in saeculum saeculi.

A good understanding have all they that do His commandments: His praise endureth for ever.

Gloria Patri, et Filio, et Spiritui Sancto.

Glory be to the Father, and to the Son, and to the Holy Ghost.

Sicut erat in principio, et nunc, et semper, et in saecula saeculorum. Amen.

As it was in the beginning, is now and ever shall be, world without end. Amen.

Antiphon with Psalm 111

Exortum est in tenebris lumen rectis corde: misericors, et miserator, et iustus Dominus.

To the true of heart a light is risen up in darkness: the Lord is merciful, and compassionate and just.

Beatus vir, qui timet Dominum: in mandatis eius volet nimis.

Blessed is the man that feareth the Lord, that delighteth greatly in His commandments.

Potens in terra erit semen eius: generatio rectorum benedicetur.

His seed shall be mighty upon earth; the generation of the upright shall be blessed.

Gloria et divitiae in dome eius: et iustitia eius manet in saeculum saeculi.

Glory and riches shall be in his house: and his righteousness endureth for ever.

Exortum est in tenebris lumen rectis: misericors, et miserator, et iustus.

Unto the upright there ariseth light in the darkness: he is gracious, and full of compassion, and righteousness.

Iucundus homo qui miseretur et commodat, disponent sermones suos in iudicio: quia in aeternum non commovebitur.

Happy is the man that showeth favour and lendeth; he will guide his words with discretion: surely he shall not be moved for ever.

In memoria aeterna erit iustus: ab auditione mala non timebit.

The righteous shall be in everlasting remembrance. He shall not be afraid of evil tidings.

Paratum cor eius sperare in Domino, confirmatum est cor eius: non commovebitur donec despiciat inimicos suos.

His heart is ready, trusting in the Lord. His heart is established, he shall not be afraid until he see his desire upon his enemies.

Dispersit, dedit pauperibus: iustitia eius manet in saeculum saeculi: cornu eius exaltabitur in gloria.

He hath dispersed, he hath given to the poor: his righteousness endureth for ever: his horn shall be exalted with honour.

Peccator videbit, et irascetur, dentibus suis fremet et tabescet: desiderium peccatorum peribit.

The wicked shall see it, and be grieved; he shall gnash his teeth, and melt away: the desire of the wicked shall perish.

Gloria Patri, et Filio, et Spiritui Sancto.

Glory be to the Father, and to the Son, and to the Holy Ghost.

Sicut erat in principio, et nunc et semper, et in saecula saeculorum. Amen.

As it was in the beginning, is now and ever shall be, world without end. Amen.

Antiphon with Psalm 129

Apud Dominum misericordia, et copiosa apud eum redemptio.

With the Lord there is mercy, and with Him plentiful redemption.

De profundis clamavi ad te, Domine: Domine, exaudi vocem meam.

Out of the depths I have cried to Thee, O Lord! Lord, hear my voice.

Fiant aures tuae intendentes: in vocem deprecationis meae.

Let Thine ears be attentive to the voice of my supplication.

Si iniquitates observaveris, Domine: Domine, quis sustinebit?

If Thou, Lord, shalt observe iniquities, Lord, who shall endure it?

Quia apud te propitiatio est: et propter legem tuam sustinui te, Domine.

For with Thee there is merciful forgiveness, and by reason of Thy law I have waited upon Thee, O Lord.

Sustinuit anima mea in verbo eius: speravit anima mea in Domino.

My soul hath relied on His word: my soul hath hoped in the Lord.

A custodia matutina usque ad noctem: speret Israel in Domino.

From the morning watch even until night let Israel hope in the Lord.

Quia apud Dominum misericordia: et copiosa apud eum redemptio.

For with the Lord there is mercy, and with Him plentiful redemption.

Et ipse redimet Israel, ex omnibus iniquitatibus eius.

And He shall redeem Israel, from all his iniquities.

Gloria Patri, et Filio, et Spiritui Sancto.

Glory be to the Father, and to the Son, and to the Holy Ghost.

Sicut erat in principio, et nunc, et semper, et in saecula saeculorum. Amen.

As it was in the beginning, is now and ever shall be, world without end. Amen.

Short Responsory

R. Verbum caro factum est,
Alleluia, alleluia.
V. Et habitavit in nobis.
Alleluia, Alleluia.
Gloria Patri, et Filio
et Spiritui Sancto.

R. The Word was made flesh,
Alleluia, alleluia.
V. And dwelt among us.
Alleluia, alleluia.
Glory be to the Father, and to the Son,
and to the Holy Ghost.

Hymn

Christe, Redemptor omnium,
Ex Patre, Patris Unice,
Solus ante principium
Natus ineffabiliter

Jesus! Redeemer of the world!
Who, ere the earliest dawn of light,
Was from eternal ages born,
Immense in glory as in might.

Tu lumen, tu splendor Patris,
Tu spes perennis omnium:
Intende, quas fundunt preces.
Tui per orbem famuli.

Immortal Hope of all mankind
In whom the Father's face we see,
Hear Thou the prayers Thy people pour
This day throughout the world to Thee.

Memento, salutis Auctor,
Quod nostri quondam corporis,

Remember, O Creator Lord!
That in the Virgin's sacred womb

Ex illibata Virgine
Nascendo, formam sumpseris.

Thou was conceiv'd and of her flesh
Didst our mortality assume.

Sic praesens testatur dies,
Currens per anni circulum,
Quod solus a sede Patris
Mundi salus adveneris.

This ever-blest recurring day
Its witness bears, that all alone,
From Thy own Father's bosom forth,
To save the world Thou camest down.

Hunc caelum, terra, hunc mare,
Hunc omne, quod in eis est,
Auctorem adventus tui
Laudans exultat cantico.

O Day! to which the seas and sky,
And earth, and heav'n, glad welcome sing;
O Day! which heal'd our misery,
And brought on earth salvation's King.

Nos quoque, qui sancto tuo,
Redempti sanguine sumus,
Ob diem natalis tui
Hymnum novum concinimus.

We, too, O Lord, who have been cleans'd
In Thy own fount of Blood divine,
Offer the tribute of sweet song
On this blest natal day of Thine.

Gloria tibi, Domine,
Qui natus es de Virgine,
Cum Patre et Sancto Spiritu
In sempiterna saecula.

O Jesu! born of Virgin bright,
Immortal glory be to Thee;
Praise to the Father infinite
And Holy Ghost eternally.

Amen

Amen.

V. Notum fecit Dominus, alleluia.
R. Salutare suum, alleluia.

V. The Lord hath made known, alleluia.
R. His salvation, alleluia.

Antiphon at the Magnificat

Hodie Christus natus est: hodie Salvator apparuit:
hodie in terra canunt Angeli, laetantur Archangeli:
hodie exsultant iusti, dicentes:
Gloria in excelsis Deo, alleluia.

This day Christ was born: this day the Saviour appeared:
this day the Angels sing on earth, and the Archangels
rejoice: this day the just exult, saying:
Glory to God in the highest, alleluia.

Magnificat anima mea Dominum.
Et exsultavit spiritus meus in Deo salutari meo.
Quia respexit humilitatem ancillae suae: ecce enim ex hoc beatam me dicent omnes generationes.
Quia fecit mihi magna qui potens est: et sanctum nomen eius.
Et misericordia eius a progenie in progenies timentibus eum.
Fecit potentiam in brachio suo: dispersit superbos mente cordis sui.

Deposuit potentes de sede, et exaltavit humiles.

My soul doth magnify the Lord.
And my spirit hath rejoiced in God my Saviour.
For He hath regarded the lowliness of His handmaid: for behold from henceforth all generations shall call me blessed.
For He that is mighty hath done great things to me: and holy is His name.
And His mercy is from generation unto generations, unto them that fear Him.
He hath showed strength with His arm: He hath scattered the proud in the imagination of their heart.
He hath put down the mighty from their seat, and hath exalted the humble.

Esurrentes implevit bonis: et divites dimisit inanes.

Suscepit Israel puerum suum, recordatus misericordiae suae.

Sicut locutus est ad patres nostros, Abraham, et semini eius in saecula.

Gloria Patri, et Filio et Spiritui Sancto.

Sicut erat in principio, et nunc, et semper, et in saecula saeculorum. Amen.

He hath filled the hungry with good things: and the rich He hath sent empty away.

He hath received Israel His servant, being mindful of His mercy.

As He spake to our forefathers, Abraham and to his seed for ever.

Glory be to the Father, and to the Son, and to the Holy Ghost.

As it was in the beginning, is now and ever shall be, world without end. Amen.

<table>
<tr><td>

Victimae paschali laudes Sequence for the Solemn Mass of Easter Day

</td><td>

3

</td></tr>
</table>

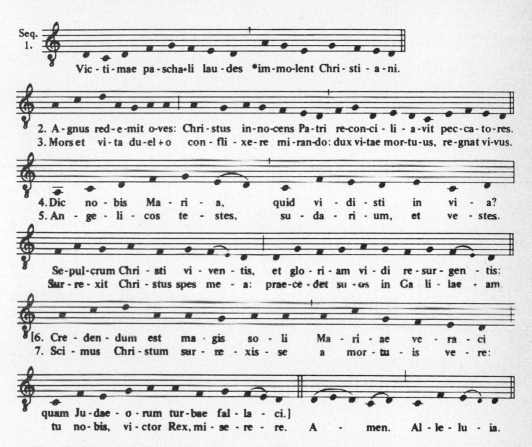

Seq. 1.
Vic - ti - mae pa - scha•li lau - des *im - mo - lent Chri - sti - a - ni.

2. A - gnus red - e - mit o - ves: Chri - stus in - no - cens Pa - tri re - con - ci - li - a - vit pec - ca - to - res.
3. Mors et vi - ta du - el ♦ o con - fli - xe - re mi - ran - do: dux vi - tae mor - tu - us, re - gnat vi - vus.

4. Dic no - bis Ma - ri - a, quid vi - di - sti in vi - a?
5. An - ge - li - cos te - stes, su - da - ri - um, et ve - stes.

Se - pul - crum Chri - sti vi - ven - tis, et glo - ri - am vi - di re - sur - gen - tis:
Sur - re - xit Chri - stus spes me - a: prae - ce - det su - os in Ga - li - lae - am.

[6. Cre - den - dum est ma - gis so - li Ma - ri - ae ve - ra - ci
7. Sci - mus Chri - stum sur - re - xis - se a mor - tu - is ve - re:

quam Ju - dae - o - rum tur - bae fal - la - ci.]
tu no - bis, vi - ctor Rex, mi - se - re - re. A - men. Al - le - lu - ia.

LU, p. 780. Reprinted from Richard Hoppin, *Anthology of Medieval Music* (New York, 1978), No. 12, p. 15.

1. Victimae paschali laudes immolent Christiani.
1. To the Paschal Victim let Christians offer songs of praise.

2. Agnus redemit oves: Christus innocens Patri reconciliavit peccatores.
2. The Lamb has redeemed the sheep. Sinless Christ has reconciled sinners to the Father.

3. Mors et vita duelo conflixere mirando: dux vitae mortuus, regnat vivus.
3. Death and life have engaged in miraculous combat. The leader of life is slain, (yet) living he reigns.

4. Dic nobis Maria, quid vidisti in via? Sepul-
   crum Christi viventis, et gloriam vidi
   resurgentis:
5. Angelicos testes, sudarium, et vestes. Sur-
   rexit Christus spes mea: praecedet
   suos in Galilaeam.
6. Credendum est magis soli Mariae veraci
   quam Judaeorum turbae fallaci.

7. Scimus Christum surrexisse a mortuis vere:
   tu nobis, victor Rex, miserere.

                        WIPO OF BURGUNDY (d. 1048?)

4. Tell us, Mary, what you saw on the way? I
   saw the sepulchre of the living Christ
   and the glory of His rising;
5. The angelic witnesses, the shroud and ves-
   ture. Christ my hope is risen. He will
   go before his own into Galilee.
6. The truthful Mary alone is more to be believed than the deceitful crowd of
   Jews.
7. We know that Christ has truly risen from
   the dead. Thou conqueror and king,
   have mercy on us.

                                      R. HOPPIN

Gloria with Trope, *Spiritus et alme* 4

Gló - ri - a in ex-cel - sis Dé - o. Et in tér - ra pax ho - mi - ni - bus bó - nae vo-lun-tá - tis.

Lau - dá - mus te. Be - ne - dí - ci - mus te. A - do - rá - mus te. Glo - ri - fi - cá - mus te.

Grá - ti - as á - gi - mus tí - bi pro-pter má - gnam gló - ri - am tú - am. Dó - mi - ne Dé - us,

Rex cae - lé - stis, Dé - us Pá - ter o - mní - po-tens. Dó - mi - ne Fí - li u - ni - gé - ni - te, Jé - su Chrí - ste.

Spí - ri - tus et ál - me or - pha - nó - rum Pa - ra - clí - te. Dó - mi - ne Dé - us, A - gnus Dé - i, Fi - li - us Pa - tris.

Pri - mo - gé - ni - tus Ma - rí - ae, vír - gi - nis Má - tris. Qui tól - lis pec - cá - ta mún - di, mi - se - ré - re nó - bis.

Qui tól - lis pec - cá - ta mún - di, sús - ci - pe de - pre - ca - ti - ó - nem nó - stram. *ad Ma - rí - ae gló - ri - am.*

Qui sé - des ad déx - te - ram Pá - tris, mi - se - ré - re nó - bis. Quó - ni - am tu só - lus sán - ctus. *Ma - rí - am san - ctí - fi - cans.*

Tu só - lus Dó - mi - nus. *Ma - rí - am gú - ber - nans.* Tu só - lus Al - tís - si - mus, *Ma - rí - am có - ro - nans.*

Jé - su Chri - ste. Cum Sán - cto Spí - ri - tu, in gló - ri - a Dé - i Pá - tris. A - men.

Gloria: *LU*, pp. 40–42; Trope: Peter Wagner, *Einführung in die Gregorianischen Melodien*, III, 510. Copyright © 1921 Breitkopf & Härtel, Leipzig. Alexander Broude, Inc., sole agent. Reprinted by permission.

Gloria in excelsis Deo.
Et in terra pax hominibus
bonae voluntatis.
Laudamus te.
Benedicimus te.
Adoramus te. Glorificamus te.
Gratias agimus tibi propter
magnam gloriam tuam.
Domine Deus, Rex caelestis,
Deus Pater omnipotens.
Domine Fili unigenite,
Jesu Christe.
Spiritus et alme orphanorum Paraclite.

Domine Deus, Agnus Dei, Filius Patris.
Primogenitus Mariae, virginis Matris.
Qui tollis peccata mundi,
miserere nobis.
Qui tollis peccata mundi,
suscipe deprecationem nostram.
Ad Mariae gloriam.
Qui sedes ad dexteram Patris

miserere nobis.
Quoniam tu solus sanctus.
Mariam sanctificans.
Tu solus Dominus.
Mariam gubernans.
Tu solus Altissimus,
Mariam coronans,
Jesu Christe.
Cum Sancto Spiritu
in gloria Dei Patris.
Amen.

Glory to God in the highest.
And on earth peace to men
of good will.
We praise thee,
we bless thee,
we adore thee, we glorify thee.
We give thanks
for thy great glory.
O Lord God, King of heaven,
God the Father almighty.
O Lord, the only begotten Son,
Jesus Christ.
Of the spirit and soul of orphans the Protector.

O Lord God, Lamb of God, Son of the Father,
first born of Mary, of the virgin mother.
Thou who takest away the sins of the world,
have mercy on us.
Thou who takest away the sins of the world,
receive our prayer
to the glory of Mary.
Thou who sittest at the right hand of the Father,
have mercy on us.
For thou only art holy,
sanctifying Mary.
thou only art the Lord,
guiding Mary.
thou only art most high,
crowning Mary
O Jesus Christ,
with the Holy Ghost,
in the glory of God the Father.
Amen.

Gloria translation from HOPPIN, *AMM*, pp. 9–10

<table>
<tr><td>

Bernart de Ventadorn (ca. *1150*–ca. *1180*)

Can vei la lauzeta mover

</td><td>

5

</td></tr>
</table>

1. Can vei la lau-ze-ta mo - ver De joi sas a - las con - tral rai,

Que s'o - blid' e·s lais - sa cha - zer Per la dous-sor c'al cor li - vai,

Ai! tans grans en-vey - a m'en ve De cui qu'eu vey - a jau - zi - on,

Me - ra - vil - has ai, car des - se Lo cor de de - zi - rer no·m fon.

The dot between two parts of a word indicates a contraction. Hendrik Van der Werf, *The Chansons of the Troubadours and Trouvères* (Utrecht, 1972), pp. 91–93.

Can vei la lauzeta mover
de joi sas alas contral rai,
que s'oblid' e·s laissa chazer
per la doussor c'al cor li vai,
ai! tan grans enveya m'en ve
de cui qu'eu veya jauzion,
meravilhas ai, car desse
lo cor de dezirer no·m fon.

When I see the lark beating
its wings joyfully against the sun's rays,
which then swoons and swoops down
because of the joy in its heart,
oh! I feel such jealousy
for all those who have the joy of love,
that I am astonished
that my heart does not immediately melt with
    desire!

Ai, las! tan cuidava saber
d'amor, e tan petit en sai,
car eu d'amar no·m posc tener
celeis don ja pro non aurai.
Tout m'a mo cor, e tout m'a me,
e se mezeis e tot lo mon;
e can se·m tolc, no·m laisset re
mas dezirer e cor volon.

Alas! I thought I knew so much
of love, and I know so little;
for I cannot help loving a lady
from whom I shall never obtain any favor.
She has taken away my heart and myself,
and herself and the whole world;
and when she left me, I had nothing left
but desire and a yearning heart.

Anc non agui de me poder
ni no fui meus de l'or' en sai
que·m laisset en sos olhs vezer

I have no power over myself,
and have not had possession of myself
since the time when she allowed me to look
    into her eyes,

en un miralh que mout me plai.
Mirahls, pus me mirei en te,
m'an mort li sospir depreon,

in a mirror which I like very much.
Mirror, since I was reflected in you,
deep sighs have killed me,

c'aissi·m perdei com perdet se
lo bels Narcisus en la fon.

for I caused my own ruin, just as
fair Narcissus caused his by looking in the
    fountain.

De las domnas me dezesper;
ja mais en lor no·m fiarai;
c'aissi com las solh chaptener,
enaissi las deschaptenrai.
Pois vei c'una pro no m'en te
vas leis que·m destrui e·m confon,
totas las dopt' e las mescre,
car be sai c'atretals se son.

I despair of ladies;
I shall not trust them ever again;
just as I used to defend them,
now I shall condemn them.
Since I see that *one* of them does not help me
against her who is ruining and destroying me
I fear them all and have no faith in them,
for I know they are all the same.

D'aisso's fa be femna parer
ma domna, par qu'e·lh o retrai,
car no vol so c'om deu voler,

My lady shows herself to be [merely] a woman
(and that is why I reproach her)
in that she does not want what one should
    want,

e so c'om li devada, fai.
Chazutz sui en mala merce,
et ai be faih co·l fols en pon;
e no sai per que m'esdeve,

and she does what is forbidden her.
I have fallen out of favor,
and have acted like the fool on the bridge;
and I do not know why this has happened to
    me,

mas car trop puyei contra mon.

unless it was because I tried to climb too high.

Merces es perduda, per ver,
et eu non o saubi anc mai,
car cilh qui plus en degr'aver
no·n a ges, et on la querrai?
A! can mal sembla, qui la ve,

Mercy is gone, that is sure,
and I never received any of it,
for she who should have the most mercy
has none, and where else should I seek it?
Oh! how difficult it is for a person who sees
    her

qued aquest chaitiu deziron

to imagine that she would allow to die this
    poor yearning wretch,

que ja ses leis non aura be,
laisse morir, que no l'aon!

and would not help the man
who can have no help but her!

Pus ab midons no·m pot valer
precs ni merces ni·l dreihz qu'eu ai,
ni a leis no ven a plazer
qu'eu l'am, ja mais no·lh o dirai.

Since pleas and mercy and my rights
cannot help me to win my lady,
and since it does not please her
that I love her, I shall speak to her about it no
    more.

Aissi·m part de leis e·m recre;
mort m'a, e per mort h respon,
e van m'en, pus ilh no·m rete,

So I am leaving her and her service;
she has killed me, and I reply with death,
and I am going sadly away, since she will not
    accept

chaitius, en issilh, no sai on.

my service, into exile, I do not know where.

Tristans, ges no·n auretz de me,
qu'eu m'en vau, chaitius, no sai on.

Tristan, you will hear no more of me,
for I am going sadly away, I do not know
    where,

De chantar me gic e·m recre,
e de joi d'amor m'escon.

I am going to stop singing,
and I flee from love and joy.

<table>
<tr><td>

Peire Vidal *(1180–ca. 1206)*
Baros, de mon dan covit

</td><td>

6

</td></tr>
</table>

Ba - ros de mon dan co - vit, Fals lau-zen-giers des - lei - als, Et eu am la_____
Qu'en tal dom-na ai chau - zit, On es fis pretz na - tu - rals, E sui totz seus,_____

de fin cor, ses bau - zi - a Quar sa beu-tatz e sa va - lors pa - reis,
quo-ra qu'ilh si mi - a, Qu'en leis a - mar fo - ra

hon - ratz us_____ reis,____ Per que·m tieng rics sol que·m deinh di - re____ d'oc.____

Adapted from Friedrich Gennrich, *Der musikalische Nachlass der Troubadours* (Darmstadt, 1958), I, 67, no. 61.

Baros de mon dan covit,	My lord, the vile slanderer rejoices
Fals lauzengiers desleials,	over the ills he may now be able to bring
	about,
Qu'en tal domna ai chauzit,	for I have chosen a lady
On es fis pretz naturals,	in whom are united all the natural virtues.
Et eu am la de fin cor, ses bauzia	I love her completely, without falsehood,
E sui totz seus, quora qu'ilh si mia,	and am entirely hers, if she will be mine.
Quar sa beutatz e sa valors pareis,	Her beauty and her worth are so great
Qu'en leis amar fora honratz us reis,	that a king would gain honor by loving her;
Per que·m tieng rics sol que·m deinh dire	thus I would hold myself rich, were she to ac-
d'oc.	cept me.

Adam de la Halle (ca. *1237*–ca. *1287*)
Jeu de Robin et de Marion: Rondeau, *Robins m'aime*

Friedrich Gennrich, *Troubadours, Trouvères, Minne – und Meistergesang* (Cologne, 1951), p. 38.

Robin m'aime,	Robin loves me,
Robin m'a,	Robin has me,
Robins m'a demandée	Robin asked me
Si m'ara.	if he can have me.
Robins m'acata cotele	Robin took off my skirt
D'escarlate bonnet et belle,	of scarlet, good and pretty,
Souskanie et chainturele.	my bodice and girdle.
Aleuriva!	Hurray!

Wizlau von Rügen (ca. *1268–1325*)
We ich han gedacht

1. We ich han ge - dacht Al di - sen nacht An mi - ne gro - zen swe - re. De eyn
2. Vil sů - ze vrucht, Wer daz din tzucht, Daz du mich wult vůr - ter - ben? Wer
3. Waz ich ye ghe - sanc, Nie mir ghe - lanc An di - ner ho - hen min - ne; Des

wip be - ghat, Un-de mich nicht lat Ko-men tzů ey - ner we - re, Daz se mir wol-de na-hen:
gna - de socht, Unn der an dir rocht, Dem solt du sel - de er - ben. Daz we-re an mi - me ra - te,
li - de ich not. Eyn ir - ren tot, Den ich da - von ghe - win - ne. I - mer wil ich dich bit-ten:

Eyn cus - se - lin Uz ir munt ist phin, Den wol - de ich wol unt - pha - hen.
Daz du min - nen phant In si - ne hant Ghe-best uz di - nes hert - zen gra - te.
Mir hilft keyn rat, Al - so mir nu stat In mi - nem hert - zen mit - ten.

Transcribed from the neumatic notation in Georg Holz, Franz Saran and Eduard Bernouilli, *Die Jenaer Liederhandschrift* (Leipzig, 1901), I, 130.

Alas, I have been thinking
this whole night
of my great burdens,
which a woman begot
and which do not allow me
to feel at all secure
that she might want to approach me:
a little kiss
from her mouth is a lovely thing,
which I would gladly accept.

Such a sweet creature,
with all your fine breeding:
yet you want to destroy me?
On him who seeks affection
and hopes for it from you
you ought to bestow happiness.
This would be my advice:
that you give love's pledge
in his hand
from your heart's midst.

Whatever I sang,
I never rose
to your nobles love:
therefore I suffer distress,
a stray death,
which I thereby achieve.
Always will I come begging to you.
No advice will help me,
as I now feel
in my heart's midst.

9 Hans Sachs (1494–1576)
Nachdem David war redlich und aufrichtig

[STOLLEN]

1. Nach — — — dem Da - vid war red - lich und auff — rich - tig
2. Sprach: "er würgt Da - vid heim - lich, gar für — sich - tig."

In al - len sach - en treu als gol — de, Do wart jm Saul gar nei - dig;
Doch war Jo - na - than Da - vid hol — de: Dem wars von her — zen lei - de;

Rett mitt all sei - nen Knecht-en in ge — dul - de. 9. Da - vid Er das an - sa - get
Das jhn Saul wollt' tö - ten ohn al - le schul - de 10. Sprach:"mein Va - ter rad-schla-get

[ABGESANG]

11. Wie Er dich heim - lich thu er - mö - ren. Dar-umb auff mor-gen. So bleib ver - bor - gen

[STOLLEN REPEATED]

Ver-steck dich auf dem fel - de." 15. So

wiel jch re - den von dem Han-del wich-tig, Was ich vom Va - ter den wertt hö — ren,

Ich dir treu - lich ver-mel - de, Ob bey jhm sey feint - schafft o - der hul - de.

Adapted from diplomatic copy in G. Münzer, *Das Singebuch des Adam Puschman* (Leipzig, 1906), p. 80. Notation in whole and half notes, some with dots, is in the original manuscript in Wroclaw, Municipal Library. Half-notes are meant to go much faster than whole notes. Dotted half-notes are somewhat prolonged. Puschman labels this *Weise* or melodic formula "Klingende Ton" (chiming or ringing mode).

Nachdem David war redlich und aufrichtig,
In allen sachen treu als golde,
Do wart jm Saul gar neidig;
Rett mit all seinen knechten in gedulde.
Sprach: "er würgt David heimlich, gar
    fürsichtig."
Doch war Jonathan David holde;
Dem wars von herzen leide,

Since David was honest and candid,
in all things true as gold,
so Saul was very jealous of him.
He dealt with all his vassals with patience.
Said he: "He struggled with David secretly,
    cautiously.
Yet Jonathan was kind to David;
it was painful to his heart

Das jhn Saul wollte töten ohn alle schulde.

David Er das ansaget,
Sprach: ''mein Vater radschlaget,
Wie Er dich heimlich thu ermören.
Darumb auff morgen,
So bleib verborgen,
Versteck dich auf dem felde.''
So wiel ich reden von dem handel wichtig,
Was ich vom Vater den wertt hören,
Ich dir treu vermelde,
Ob bey ihm sey feintschaft oder hulde.

that Saul wanted to kill him [David] without
any blame.
Thus he spoke to David:
saying, ''My father turned a somersault,
when he secretly [planned] to murder you;
therefore in the morning
remain concealed,
hide yourself in the field.''
As much as I tell of the affair is important;
what I, concerning the father's honor, heard,
I truthfully impart,
whether there was hostility in him or kindness.

10 Istampita Palamento

f. 60r.

Prima pars

Jan ten Bokum, *De Dansen* (Utrecht, 1976), pp. 49–50. Facsimile in Gilbert Reaney ed., *The Manuscript London, British Museum, Additional 29987* (American Institute of Musicology, 1965), fols. 60r–61v.

11   *Alleluia Justus ut palma* (ca. *1100*)

[Soloists] Al-le - lu - ia   [Choir] Al-le - lu - ia.

[Soloists] Ius - tus   ut pal - ma   flo - re - bit

et si - cut ce - - - - - - - - - -

- - drus mul - ti - pli-ca - bi - tur.

[Choir]

Milan, Biblioteca Ambrosiana, MS M.17 sup., ed. Hans Heinrich Eggebrecht and Frieder Zaminer, *Ad organum facien-dum, Lehrschriften der Mehrstimmigkeit in nachguidonischer Zeit* (Mainz, 1970), p. 53.

Alleluia Justus ut palma florebit,
et sicut cedrus multiplicabitur.

Alleluia. The righteous shall flourish
like a palm tree and shall multiply like a cedar.

Versus: *Senescente mundano filio*

12

Se - ne - scen - te mun - da - no fi - li - o /

Quem fo-ve-bat men - tis o - bli - vi -

o / Ve - nit spon-sus di-vi-na ra - ti - o /

Co - mes e - ius est re-stau - ra - ci -

- o / So - la vir - go re -

ga - lis fi - li - a / Di - gna di - gnis pa-rat hos-pi-ci - a /

Transcribed by Sarah Ann Fuller from Paris, Bibliothèque Nationale, MS lat. 3549, fol. 153.
(♪) denotes no fixed durational value. Notes flagged together belong to the same ligature. (♪) is a plica, and (/) indicates the end of a poetic line. Notes in brackets have been supplied.

Ap-ta co-mes re-plet pa-la-ti - a / Au-lam spon-sus in-trat per ho- sti - a.

Senescente mundano filio	While the earthly son grows old
Quem fovebat mentis oblivio	whom forgetfulness was favoring,
Venit sponsus divina ratio	comes the bridegroom, divine reason.
Comes eius est restauracio.	His companion is refreshment.
Sola virgo regalis filia	Sole virgin, royal daughter,
Digna dignis para hospitia	prepare guest chambers worthy of the deserving;
Apta comes replet palacia	a fitting companion fills the palaces.
Aulam sponsus intrat per hostia.	The bridegroom enters the hall through the doors.

<table>
<tr><td>

Alleluia Pascha nostrum Gregorian chant
and early polyphony based on it

</td><td>

13

</td></tr>
</table>

a) Alleluia Pascha nostrum, *plainchant*

Gordon A. Anderson, *The Latin Compositions in Fascicules VII and VIII of the Notre Dame Manuscript Wolfenbüttel Helmstadt 1099,* Part II, p. 276. Réproduit avec permission de l'Institut de musique médiévale, Henryville, Ottawa et Binningen

b) Leonin, (fl. *1160–1180*) Organum duplum, *Alleluia pascha nostrum*

Florence, Biblioteca Medicea-Laurenziana, MS pluteus 29.1, fol. 109; the clausulae are from Anderson, II, 25–26.

c) *Conductus-motet on Leonin's clausula on* nostrum

Triplum

Duplum

Gau - de - at de - vo - ti - o fi - de - li - um; Ver - bum pa - tris in - car - na - tur,

Cantus

Nostrum.

No - va pro - les no - bis da - tur Et no - bis - cum con - ver - sa - tur Sa - lus gen - ti - um. Vi - te pan - dit

o - sti - um, Dum mor-tis sup -pli - ci - um, Pi - e to - le - rat. Mun-di prin-ceps ex -tur-ba-tur,

Dum con-si - de - rat, Quod per mor-tem li - be-ra-tur Qui per-i - e - rat, Iu - re su - o

sic pri-va-tur, Dum de-si - de - rat Il -lum si - bi sub-de-re, qui nil com-mi - se - rat.

Anderson, II, 25–26.

d) *Substitute clausula on* nostrum

Florence, MS pluteus 29.1, fol. 157v, ed. Anderson, II, 199–200.

e) *Motet,* Salve, salus hominum—O radians stella—nostrum

Triplum: Sal - ve, sa - lus ho-mi - num, Spes mi-se - ri - cor-di - e,
Duplum: O ra-di - ans stel-la pre ce-te - ris, Sum - mi De - i ma-ter
Cantus: Nostrum.

Spes ve-ni - e, Pur-ga - trix cri-mi - num, Ce - cis lu - men lu - mi - num,
et fi - li - a, E - xi-mi - a pro-les de - ge-ne - ris, Tu ge-ne-

Ma - ter, pru - den-ti - e, Si - gnum vi - e, Ter-mi - nus pa-tri-
ris Mun-di le - ti - ti - a, Tu de vi - a tri-bu - los con-te - ris,

e, Spes ve-ni - e, Ne-ctar, flos glo-ri - e, Iu - sti-ti - e Sol pi-
Spes mi-se - ris, Ho-mi - nis Ne-sci - a, Ma-ri - a, De la-te - ris lu-to

e, Cle - men-ti - e So-bri - e Ros, vir-go mun - di-ti - e.
nos li-be - ra, Re - ge-ne - rans ge-nus in po-ste - ris re-gi - a.

Anderson, II, 199–200.

b) Leonin, Organum duplum, *Alleluia pascha nostrum*

f) *Motet,* Ave Maria, Fons letitie—latus *on Leonin's clausula on* latus

Anderson, II, 73–76.

b) Leonin, Organum duplum, *Alleluia pascha nostrum*

g) *Motet*, Qui d'amors veut bien—Qui longuement porroit—nostrum *on substitute clausula on* nostrum *(13d)*

Hans Tischler, *The Earliest Motets* (New Haven, in press), Motet 137–1. Printed by permission.

a) Alleluia. Pascha nostrum immolatus   Alleluia. Christ, our paschal lamb, is sacri-
   est Christus.   fied.

c) Gaudeat devotio fidelium;   Let the devotion of the faithful be raised in
   Verbum patris incarnatur,   rejoicing;
   Nova proles nobis datur   the word of the father is made flesh,
   Et nobis cum conversatur   and a new child is given to us,
   Salus gentium.   and He has bestowed Himself upon us.
   Vite pandit ostium,   The salvation of the people
   Dum mortis supplicium,   has opened the gateway of life,
   Pie tolerat.   for he in devotion has borne
   Mundi princeps exturbatur,   the punishment of death.
   Dum considerat,   Satan was cast down
   Quod per morten liberatur   when He stood firm
   Qui perierat.   so that through His death
   Iure suo sic privatur,   he who had perished might be made free;
   Dum desiderat   thus was He stripped of His own divine nature
   Illum sibi subdere, qui nihil commiserat.   when He, unflinching,
                                               chose to subdue death unto Himself—He who
                                                  had committed no sin.

Triplum

e) Salve, salus hominum,   Hail, safety of men,
   Spes misericordie,   hope of pity,
   Spes venie,   hope of pardon,
   Purgatric criminum,   cleanser of sins,
   Cecis lumen luminum,   light of light to the blind,
   Mater prudentie,   Mother of prudence,
   Signum vie,   sign-post of the way,
   Terminus patrie,   boundary of Heaven,
   Spes venie,   hope of pardon,
   Nectar, flos glorie,   nectar, flower of glory,
   Iustitie   of justice,
   Sol pie,   holy sun,
   Clementie   of temperate
   Sobrie   Purgatrix
   Ros, virgo munditie.   dew, Virgin of cleanliness!

Adapted from ANDERSON, II, 324.

Duplum

O radians stella pre ceteris,   O shining star, outshining all others,
Summi Dei mater et filia,   Mother and Daughter of the highest God,
Eximia proles degeneris,   peerless offspring of a degenerate race,
Tu generis Mundi letitia,   Thou art the joy of the people of the world.
Tu de via tribulos conteris,   Thou turnest away the perils of the way.
Spes miseris,   O hope of wretched
Hominis   Man;
Nescia Maria   Mary, not knowing [the touch of man],
De lateris luto nos libera,   free us from the mire surrounding us,
Regenerans genus in posteris regia.   regenerating the human race THY KING-
                                                 DOM FOR ALL AGES.

f) Ave Maria,
  Fons letitie,
  Virgo pura, pia,
  Vas munditie,
  Te voce varia
  Sonet sobrie
  Gens leta sobria.
  Gaudens varie
  Promat ecclesia
  Laudes Marie,
  Vox ecclesie.
  Sonet in maria.
  Hec solvit scrinia
  Ysaie,
  Reserans ostia
  Clausa patrie,
  Via dans eximia
  Regem glorie,
  Qui sola gratia,
  Plenus gratie,
  Factus est hostia,
  Finis hostie.

Hail Mary,
fount of Joy,
virgin pure and holy,
vessel of chastity,
may the joyous people
sing Thee in various
yet restrained voices.
Rejoicing for many blessings,
let the Church express
its praise for Mary;
and let the voice of the Church
resound in the sea.
She has fulfilled the prophecies
of Isaiah,
unlocking the once-closed
gates of heaven,
granting access by a wonderful way
to the King of Glory,
who by grace alone,
and full of grace,
was made sacrifice,
the end of all sacrifice.

ANDERSON, II, 52-53

Triplum

g) Qui d'amors veut bien joir
  Et gueredon en atent,
  Ne la doit pas longuement maintenir.
  Qui la maintient longuement,
  Por tant que repentir
  A son voloir ne s'en puet maintenant;
  Lors l'en doit bien celui por fol tenir;
  Car on voit bien avenir,
  Que cil qui meins i atent
  Plus i recuevre souvent.

He who wishes to enjoy love
and awaits its reward
must not for a long time
keep waiting;
he who does so for a long time
has not now the opportunity
to repent for his excesses.
One can scarcely consider him a fool for it,
for it is easy to see in the future
that he who least expects it
will regain it most often.

Duplum

Qui longuement porroit joir d'amors,
Il n'est deduit, qui mieuz vausist d'amer;

Mais l'en i a souvent larmes et plors,
Et quant en i cuide joie trover,
Lors n'i trove ne solas ne secors,
Qui amors veut sans faintise esprover,

A tous jors
Face semblant, qu'au cuer n'en ait doulor;

Si en porra joir et recouvrer
Les douçors.

He who would enjoy love for a long time,
hath no pleasure which is more worthwhile
    than love;
but there are often tears and crying in it,
And when one thinks of finding joy in it,
then one finds no solace or help.
He who wants to experience love without de-
    ceit,
For ever
Let him pretend that he has no grief in his
    heart:
And he will be able to enjoy and regain the
    sweetness of it.

Adapted from **ANDERSON**, II, 324–25.

<table>
<tr><td>14</td><td>**Perotin** *(1183?–1238?)*
Organum quadruplum: *Sederunt* Gradual
for St. Stephen's Day, Respond only</td></tr>
</table>

Reprinted from Hoppin, *AMM* No. 35, pp. 59–66.

de -

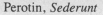

runt.

Chorus

prin - ci - pes,   et ad-ver-sum me   lo - que - ban - tur:

et In - i - qui per se cu - ti   sunt me

The rulers were seated in council, and they spoke against me; and my enemies
persecuted me.

R. HOPPIN

15 Conductus: *Ave virgo virginum*
(*13th-century*)

A - ve vir - go vir - gi - num Ver - bi car - nis cel - la,

In sa - lu - tem ho - mi - num Stil - lans lac et mel - la.

Pe - pe - ri - sti do - mi - num, Mo - y - si fi - cel - la,

O ra - di - o Sol ex - it, et lu - mi - num, fon - tem pa - rit stel - la.

Florence, Biblioteca Laurenziana, MS Pluteus 29.1, fol. 240r–240v.

Ave virgo virginum
Verbi carnis cella,
In salutem hominum
Stillans lac et mella.
Peperisti dominum,
Moysi ficella,
O radio
Sol exit, et luminum
Fontem parit stella.

Ave, plena gratia,
Caput Zabulonis
Contrivisti spolia
Reparans predonis.
Celi rorans pluvia
Vellus Gedconis,
O filio
Tu nos reconcilia,
Mater Salomonis.

Virgo tu mosayce
Rubus visionis,
De te fluxit sylice
Fons redemptionis.
Quos redemit calice
Christus passionis,
O gaudio
Induat glorifice
Resurrectionis

Hail, virgin of virgins,
shrine of the word made flesh,
who for man's salvation
drips milk and honey.
You bore the Lord;
you were a rush-basket for Moses;
O, from your rays
the sun goes forth, and the star
brings forth a fountain of light.

Hail, full of grace,
chief of Zebulun,
the spoils of robbers
you restore.
Like rain, falling from heaven
on the fleece of Gideon,
with your son
reunite us,
O mother of Solomon!

You, Virgin,
bramble-bush of the Mosaic vision,
from you flowed the fountain
through the rock of redemption.
Those Christ has redeemed through the chalice
of his passion,
O, may he clothe them with the joy
of his glorious
resurrection.

16

Motet: *Aucun vont—Amor qui cor—Kyrie* (*late 13th century*)

Au-cun vont so-vent Por lor en-vi-e Mes-di-sant d'a-mur, Mais ilh n'est si bo-ne vi-e Com

A - mor___ qui cor___ vul - ne -

1) Kyrie eleison*

d'a-mer loi - au - ment; Car d'a-meir vient to-te cor-toi-si - e,

rat Hu - ma - num, quem ge - ne -

Tote ho-nur Et tos biens en-sen - gne - mens. Tot ce puet en li

rat Car - na - lis af - fe - cti - o,

Reprinted from Hoppin, *AMM* No. 54, pp. 112–15.

gent.   Mais ver chas - cun   s'u - mi -lie Et pa-rol - le cor-toi - se -

Res   que   ci - to   la - bi -   tur

ment   S'ilh at dou tot, sens   par - ti - e, Mis sun cuer en a - meir en-tie - re -

Vel   trans - it,   e   o   mi -   nus

ment.   Et sa - chies k'ilh n'ai - me mie, Ains ment, Si silh soi   de-mainne au-tre-ment.

Di - li - ga - tur   Do -   mi -   nus.

Triplum

Aucun vont sovent	Some, through envy,
Por lor envie	often speak
Mesdisant d'amur,	ill of love;
Mais ilh n'est si bone vie	But there is no life so good
Com d'amer loiaument;	as loving loyally.
Car d'ameir vient tote cortoisie,	For from loving comes all courtesy,
Tote honur	all honor,
Et tos biens ensengnemens.	and all good breeding.
Tot ce puet en li proveir ki amie	All this can one experience

Wet faire sens boisdie
Et ameir vraiement,
Car ja en li n'iert assise
Vilonie Ne convoitise
D'amasseir argent,
Ains aime bune compagnie
Et despent ades largement,
Et si n'at en li felonie
N'envie
Sor autre gent.

Mais ver chascun s'umilie
Et parolle cortoisement
S'ilh at dou tot, sens partie,
Mis sun cuer en ameir entierement.
Et sachies k'ilh n'aime mie,
Ains ment,
Si silh soi demainne autrement.

who wishes without falseness to have
a lover and to love truly;
for never in him will there be
villany or covetousness
to amass money.
But he loves good company
and spends freely;
and in him is no treachery
nor envy
of others.

But he is humble to all
and speaks courteously,
if he has wholly, without division,
given his heart entirely to loving.
And you may know that he loves not at all,
but lies,
if he conducts himself otherwise.

Duplum

Amor qui cor vulnerat
Humanum, quem generat
Carnalis affectio,
Numquam sine vicio
Vel raro potest esse,
Quoniam est necesse
Ex quo plus diligitur
Res que cito labitur
Vel transit, eo minus
Diligatur Dominus.

Love that wounds
the human heart,
that carnal affection generates,
can never or rarely,
be without vice,
since necessarily,
the more a thing that
quicky escapes or passes
is loved, the less
the Lord is loved.

R. HOPPIN

17

Philippe de Vitry *(1291–1361)*
Motet from *Roman de Fauvel: Garrit gallus—In nova fert—Neuma*

Reprinted from Hoppin, *AMM* No. 59, pp. 120–26.

A2. I

Triplum

The cock babbles, lamenting sorrowfully,
for the whole assembly of cocks*
mourns because, while serving vigilantly,
it is trickily betrayed by the satrap.
And the fox,† like a grave robber,
thriving with the astuteness of Belial,
rules as a monarch with the consent
of the lion himself.‡ Ah, what slavery!
Lo, once again Jacob's family
is exiled by another Pharaoh.
Not, as formerly, able to escape
to the homeland of Judah, they weep.
Stricken by hunger in the desert,
lacking the help of arms,
although they cry out, they are robbed;
perhaps speedily they will die.
O harsh voice of the wretched exiles;
O sorrowfully babbling of the cocks,
since the dark blindness of the lion
submits to the fraud of the traitorous fox.
You who suffer the arrogance of his misdeeds,
rise up,
or what you have of honor is being or
will be lost, because if avengers are slow
men soon turn to evil doing.

* Gallus: cock; or Gauls (the French)

† Enguerran de Marigny, chief councillor of the French king

‡ Philip IV the Fair

Duplum

My heart is set upon speaking of forms
changed into new (bodies).§
The evil dragon that renowned Michael once
utterly defeated by the miraculous power
of the Cross,
now endowed with the grace of Absalom,
now with the cheerful eloquence of Ulysses,
now armed with wolfish teeth
a soldier in the service of Thersites,
lives again changed into a fox
whose tail the lion deprived
of sight obeys, while the fox reigns.
He sucks the blood of sheep and is satiated
with chickens.
Alas, he does not cease sucking and still
thirsts;
he does not abstain from meats at the wedding
feast.
Woe now to the chickens, woe to the blind
lion.
In the presence of Christ, finally, woe to
the dragon.

R. HOPPIN

§ Ovid *Metamorphoses,* 1,1.

18

Jacopo da Bologna (*14th century*)
Madrigal: *Fenice fù*

FL

Fe - ni - ce_____ fu'_____ e_____ vis - si pu - ra e

Fe - ni - ce fu' e vis - si pu - ra e

mor - - - bi - da, Et or son trasmu-ta-ta in u - na

mor - - - bi - da, Et or son tras-mu - ta-ta in u - na tor -

tor - - - - to - ra Che vo - lo con A -

- - - to - ra Che vo - lo con A-

mor___ per___ le___ bel l'or - - - - - -

mor per le bel l'or - - - - - -

- - to - ra. R. Tal_____ vis-si e tal___me vi - vo e pos-so

to - ra. R. Tal_____ vis-si e tal me vi - vo e pos-so

scri - ve - re Ch'a donna non è più chè o - ne-sta vi ve - re.

scri - ve - re___Ch'a donna non è_____ più che o - ne-sta vi - ve - re.

Nino Pirrotta, ed. *The Collected Works of Jacobo da Bologna and Vincenzo da Rimini* (American Institute of Musicology, 1963), p. 6. Reprinted by permission of A. Carapetyan, Director and Hänssler-Verlag, West Germany. All rights reserved. International copyright secured. Reprinted by permission.

Fenice fù e vissi pura e morbida,
Et or son trasmutat' in una tortora,
Che vollo con amor per le belle ortora

Arbor[e] secho [mai] n'aqua torbida,
No' me deleta may per questo dubito,
Va ne l'astate l'inverno vende subito.
Tal vissi e tal me vivo e posso scrivere
C'ha donna non è più chè honesta vivere.

A phoenix was I who lived pure and tender
and now am transformed into a turtle-dove
that flies with love through the beautiful orchards, [and]
the dry woods [but] never in muddy waters.
It gives me no pleasure because of this doubt.
Go in the summer; winter comes quickly.
So I lived and so I live and can write,
which, for a woman, is no more than to live honestly.

19 Francesco Landini *(1325?–97)*
Ballata: *Non avrà ma' pietà*

Leo Schrade, ed., *Polyphonic Music of the Fourteenth Century*, IV (Paris: Oiseau Lyre, 1958), 144–45. Reprinted by permission.

Non avrà ma' pietà questa mia donna.
Se tu non faj, amore,
Ch'ella sia certa del mio grande ardore.
S'ella sapesse quanta pena i' porto
Per onestà celata nella mente
Sol per la sua bellecca, che conforto
D'altro non prende l'anima dolente,
Forse da lej sarebbono in me spente
Le fiamme che la pare
Di giorno in giorno acrescono'l dolore.

She will never have mercy, this lady of mine,
If you do not see to it, love,
that she is certain of my great ardor.
If she knew how much pain I bear—
for honesty's sake concealed in my mind—
only for her beauty, other than which
nothing gives comfort to a grieving soul,
perhaps by her would be extinguished in me
the flames which seem to arouse in
her from day to day more pain.

20

Guillaume de Machaut (ca. *1300–77*)
Double ballade: *Quant Theseus—Ne quier veoir*

[Cantus I]

I Quant The _ _ _ se _ us, Her _ _ cu _ les
Pour ac _ _ _ crois _ tre leur pris et

[Cantus II]

II Ne quier ve _ oir la biau _ te
Ne es _ prou _ ver la for _ ce

Contratenor

Tenor

et Ja _ son Cer _ _ _ cherent tout,
leur re _ non Et pour ve _ oir

d'Ab _ sa _ lon Ne de U _ li _ xes
de San _ son, Ne re _ gar _ der

et tetre et mer par _ fon _ _ _ _ _
bien tout l'es _ tat dou mon _ _ _ _ _

le sens et la fa _ con _
que Da _ li _ la le ton _

Leo Schrade, ed., *The Works of Guillaume de Machaut,* in *Polyphonic Music of the Fourteenth Century,* III (Paris: Oiseau Lyre, 1956), 124–27. Reprinted by permission.

78

Quant Theseus, Hercules et Jason
Chercherent tout, et terre et mer parfonde,
Pour accroistre leur pris et leur renon
Et pour veoir bien tout l'estat dou monde,
Moult furent dignes d'onnour.
Mais quant je voy de biauté l'umble flour,
Assevis sui de tout, si que, par m'ame,
Je voy assés, puis que je voy ma dame.

Ne quier veoir la biauté d'Absalon
Ne de Ulixés le sens et la faconde,
Ne esprouver la force de Sanson,
Ne regarder que Dalila le tonde,
Ne cure n'ay par nul tour
Des yeus Argus ne de joie gringnour,
Car pour plaisance et sans aide d'ame,

Je voy assés, puis que je voy ma dame.

When Theseus, Hercules and Jason
sought everywhere over land and deep sea
to enhance their valor and reknown
and to view fully the state of the world,
they were most worthy of honor.
But when I see of beauty a humble flower,
I am entirely content, for upon my soul,
I see enough, when I see my lady.

I am not curious to see the beauty of Absalom
or Ulysses' wisdom and eloquence,
or try the strength of Samson,
or see Dalilah cut his locks.
I do not care at all
for Argus' eyes nor any rare joy,
because for my pleasure, and with no one's
    help
I see enough, when I see my lady.

21 Guillaume de Machaut
Mass: *Agnus Dei*

Edited by Elizabeth Keitel for "Early Musical Masterworks." Printed by permission of the University of North Carolina at Chapel Hill, Department of Music.

Ag- - - - nus de- -

Ag- - - - nus de- -

Ag- - nus de- -

Ag- - - - nus de-

- - i qui tol- -

- - i qui tol- - -

- - i qui tol -

- - i qui tol- - - -

- lis pec- - ca- -

- lis pec- ca-

lis pec- - ca- ta

lis pec- - ca- ta

For translation of the text see p. 15.

Solage (*late 14th century*)
Rondeau: *Fumeux fume*

22

Willi Apel, ed. *French Secular Music of the Late Fourteenth Century,* (Mediaeval Academy of America, 1950), 64. Reprinted by permission.

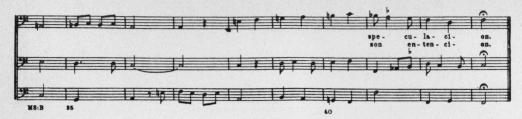

Fumeux fume par fumee
Fumeuse speculacion.
Qu'antre fummet sa pensee
Fumeux fume par fumee.

Quar fumer molt li agree
Tant qu'il ait son entencion.
Fumeux fume par fumee
Fumeuse speculacion.

Smoky fumes through smoke,
smoky speculation.
When another smokes his thoughts,
Smoky fumes through smoke.

For smoking certainly agrees with him,
as long as he gets what he wants.
Smoky fumes through smoke
smoky speculation.

Rondellus motet from Worcester:
Fulget coelestis curia

23

Luther Dittmer, *The Worcester Fragments* (American Institute of Musicology, 1957), pp. 49–50. Reprinted by permission of A. Carapetyan, Director and Hänssler-Verlag, West Germany. All rights reserved. International copyright secured. Reprinted by permission.

det de ta li prae-su le   Da to di vi no mu ne re.

ae; Du cens ad su pe ra.   No-stra cor-da fo-

re.   Ful get coe les tis cu ri a Pe tro se den te prae si de sub

Plau-dat or-bis cum glo-ri a Pe tro pri ....

ve lae ti ti a;   Prae be prae-

po li prin-ci pe

Cunc-ta a mor-ta li cri mi nae.

si di a.   No-stro-rum sce-le rum tol le ma li ti am a sum-mo

Sol ven-di cri mi na   Prae-

Sol ven-di Sor di da   Pe-

prin-ci pe No bis im-plo ra ve ni am ....

be prae si di a   Plau-dat or bis cum glo-ri a Pe tro pri vi le gi-

tre tu no bis res-pi ce   E a no-bis de i ce quae sunt ob-nox-i a.

Nos de-duc ad sum-ma gau di a.

a Por-tan te cun-cta a mor ta li cri mi ne.

Tenor 1

Fulget coelestis curia
Petro sedente praeside
Sub poli principe:
Roma gaudet de tali praesule
Dato divino munere
Plaudat orbis cum gloria
Petro pri[vilegia
Portante] cuncta a mortali criminae.
Solvendi sordida,
Petre tu nobis respice
Ea nobis deice
Quae sunt obnoxia.

Heaven's court shines forth,
with Peter sitting as guard
under the Prince of Heaven.
Rome delights in such a bishop,
granted by divine gift.
Let the earth resound with glory,
while Peter delivers the privileged
from mortal sin.
Absolving sin,
Peter, have regard for us:
cast away from us those things
that are reprehensible.

Tenor 2

O Petre flos apostolorum
Pastor coelestis curiae,
Oves pasce mellifluc;
Ducens ad supera
Nostra corda fove laetitia;
Praebe praesidia.
Nostrorum scelerum tolle malitiam
A summo principe
Nobis implora veniam
Nos deduc ad summa guadia.

O Peter, flower of the apostles,
shepherd of the heavenly court,
nourish your sheep sweetly,
leading them to higher things.
Our hearts, warm up with gladness;
grant us protection.
Bear the iniquity of our evil deeds.
From the highest prince
beg for us mercy;
lead us away to supreme joys.

Tenor 3

Roma gaudet de tali pracsule
Dato divino munere.
Fulget coeslestis curia
Petro sedente praeside
Sub poli principe.
Solvendi crimina
Praebe praesidia.
Plaudat orbis cum gloria
Petro privilegia
Portante cuncta a mortali crimine.

Rome delights in such a bishop,
granted by divine gift.
Heaven's court shines forth,
with Peter sitting as guard
under the Prince of Heaven.
Absolving our sins,
Grant us protection
Let the world resound with glory,
while Peter delivers the privileged
from mortal sin.

24

Carol: *Salve, sancta parens*
(*15th century*)

John Stevens, ed., *Mediaeval Carols*, Musica Britannica, IV (London: Stainer & Bell, 1952), 71. Reprinted by permission.

Salve, sancta parens,
Enixa puerpera Regem.
Salve, porta paradisi,
Felix atque fixa,
Stella fulgens in sublimi
Sidus enixa.

Hail, holy parent,
from a woman in labor issued a King.
Hail, gate of paradise,
happy and firm,
star shining on high
from which a constellation sprang.

25

John Dunstable (ca. *1385–1453*)
Motet: *Quam pulchra es*

Reprinted from Donald J. Grout, *History of Western Music,* revised edition, (New York, 1973), pp. 155–56.

as - si - mi - la - ta est pal - - - me,   et u - be - ra

si - mi - la - ta est pal - - - me,   et u - be - ra

si - mi - la - ta est pal - - - me,   et u - be - ra

tu - a bo - tris.   Ca - put tu - um   ut Car - me - lus,

tu - a bo - tris. Ca - put   tu - um ut   Car - me - lus,

tu - a bo - tris.   Ca - put   tu - um ut Car - - me - lus, col -

col - lum tu - um si - cut   tur - - ris   e - bur -

col - lum tu - um si - cut tur - - ris   e - bur -

col - lum tu - um si - cut tur - - ris   e - - bur -

Quam pulchra es et quam decora,
    carissima in delicis.
Statuta tua assimilata est palme,
    et ubera tua botris.
Caput tuum ut Carmelus,
    collum tuum sicut turis eburnea.
Veni, dilecte mi,
    egrediamur in agrum,
et videamus si flores fructus parturierunt
    si floruerunt mala Punica.
Ibi dabo tibi ubera mea.
Alleluia.

How fair and how pleasant art thou,
    O love, for delights!
Thy stature is like to a palm tree, and
    thy breasts to clusters of grapes.
Thine head upon thee is like Carmel;
    thy neck is a tower of ivory.
Come, my beloved,
    let us go forth into the field . . .
And see whether the tender grapes appear and
    the pomegranates bud forth:
There will I give thee my loves.
Alleluia.

D. GROUT

Guillaume Dufay (ca. *1400–74*)
Hymn: *Conditor alme siderum* (even verses, alternating with plainchant)

26

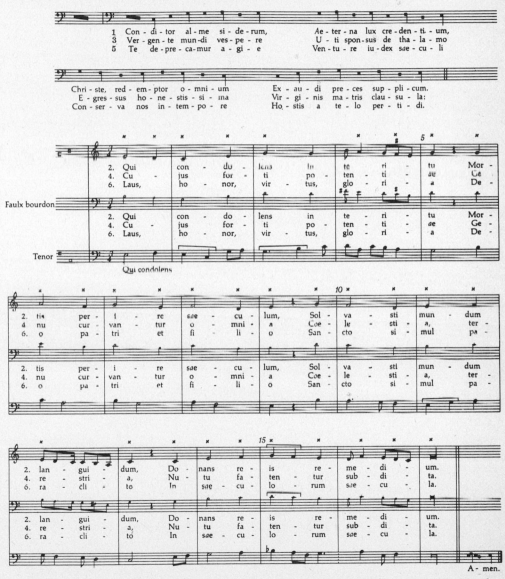

1 Con - di - tor al - me si - de - rum,   Ae - ter - na lux cre - den - ti - um,
3 Ver - gen - te mun - di ves - pe - re   U - ti spon - sus de tha - la - mo
5 Te de - pre - ca - mur a - gi - e   Ven - tu - re iu - dex sae - cu - li

Chri - ste, red - em - ptor o - mni - um   Ex - au - di pre - ces sup - pli - cum.
E - gres - sus ho - ne - stis - si - ma   Vir - gi - nis ma - tris clau - su - la:
Con - ser - va nos in - tem - po - re   Ho - stis a te - lo per - ti - di.

Faulx bourdon

2. Qui con - do - lens in - te - ri - tu Mor-
4. Cu - jus for - ti po - ten - ti - ae Ge-
6. Laus, ho - nor, vir - tus, glo - ri - a De-

Tenor

Qui condolens

2. tis per - i - re sae - cu - lum, Sol - va - sti mun - dum
4. nu cur - van - tur o - mni - a Coe - le - sti - a, ter-
6. o pa - tri et fi - li - o San - cto si - mul pa-

2. lan - gui - dum, Do - nans re - is re - me - di - um.
4. re - stri - a, Nu - tu fa - ten - tur sub - di - ta.
6. ra - cli - to In sae - cu - lo - rum sae - cu - la.

A - men.

Chant from *Antiphonale,* Appendix, pp. 11–12. Dufay, *Opera omnia,* ed. Heinrich Besseler, V (American Institute of Musicology, 1966), p. 39. Reprinted by permission of A. Carapetyan, Director and Hänssler-Verlag, West Germany.

Conditor alme siderum,
Aeterna lux credentium,
Christe redemptor omnium
Exaudi preces supplicum.

Qui condolens interitu
Mortis perire saeculum,
Solvasti mundum languidum,
Donans reis remedium:

Vergente mundi vespere
Uti sponsus de thalamo,
Egressus honestissima
Virginis matris clausula:

Cujus forti potentiae
Genu curvantur omnia
Coelestia, terrestria,
Nutu fatentur subdita.

Te deprecamur agie
Venture judex saeculi
Conserva nos in tempore
Hostis a telo perfidi.

Laus, honor, virtus, gloria
Deo patri, et filio,
Sancto simul paraclito
in saeculorum saecula.

Bountiful creator of the stars,
eternal light of believers,
Christ, redeemer of all,
hear the prayers of the supplicants.

You who suffer the ruin
of death, the perishing of the race,
who saved the sick world,
bringing the healing balm.

As the world turns toward evening,
the bridegroom from his chamber
issues forth from the most chaste
cloister of the Virgin mother.

You, before whose mighty power
all bend their knees,
celestial, terrestrial,
confessing subjection to his command.

We entreat you, holy
judge of the days to come,
save us in time
from the weapons of the perfidious.

Praise, honor, courage, glory,
to God, the Father, and Son,
and also to the Holy Protector,
time everlasting, amen.

Guillaume Dufay
Motet: *Nuper rosarum flores* (1436)

27

Ter - ri - bi - lis est* lo - cus i - ste:

etc.

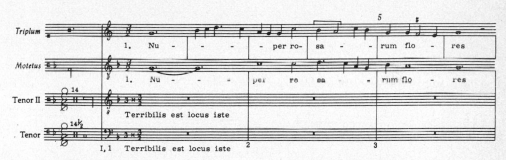

Triplum

1. Nu - - - per ro - sa - - rum flo - res

Motetus

1. Nu - - - per ro - sa - - rum flo - res

Tenor II

Terribilis est locus iste

Tenor

I, 1 Terribilis est locus iste

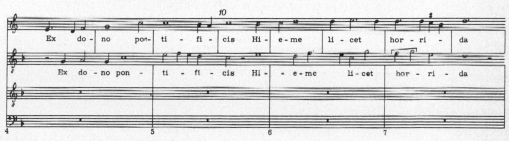

Ex do - no pon - ti - fi - cis Hi - e - me li - cet hor - ri - da

Ex do - no pon - ti - fi - cis Hi - - e - me li - cet hor - ri - da

Ti - - - bi, vir - go coe - li - ca, Pi - e et san -

Ti - - - bi, vir - go coe - li - ca, Pi - e et

This motet was composed for the consecration of the Cathedral of Santa Maria del Fiore in Florence by Pope Eugene IV on March 25, 1436. Chant from *LU*, p. 1250. Dufay, *Opera omnia*, ed. Heinrich Besseler, I (American Institute of Musicology, 1966), 70–75. Reprinted by permission of A. Carapetyan, Director and Hänssler-Verlag, West Germany. All rights reserved. International copyright secured. Reprinted by permission.

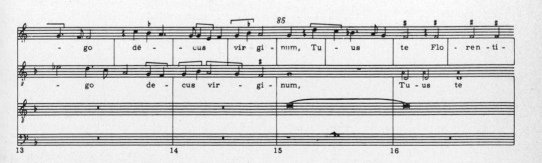

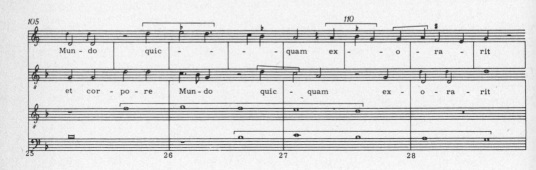

Nuper rosarum flores
Ex dono pontificis
Hieme licet horrida,
Tibi, virgo coelica,
Pie et sancte deditum
Grandis templum machinae
Condecorarunt perpetim.

Hodie vicarius
Jesu Christi et Petri
Successor EUGENIUS
Hoc idem amplissimum
Sacris templum manibus
Sanctisque liquoribus
Consecrare dignatus est.

Igitur, alma parens,
Nati tui et filia,
Virgo decus virginum,
Tuus te FLORENTIAE
Devotus orat populus,
Ut qui mente et corpore
Mundo quicquam exoravit,

Oratione tua
Cruciatus et meritis
Tui secundum carnem

Nati domini sui
Grata beneficia
Veniamque reatum
Accipere mereatur.
Amen.

Recently roses [came]
as a gift of the Pope,
although in cruel winter,
to you, heavenly Virgin.
Dutifully and blessedly is dedicated
[to you] a temple of magnificent design.
May they together be perpetual ornaments.

Today the Vicar
of Jesus Christ and Peter's
successor, Eugenius,
this same most spacious
sacred temple with his hands
and with holy waters
he is worthy to consecrate.

Therefore, gracious mother
and daughter of your offspring,
Virgin, ornament of virgins,
your, Florence's, people
devoutly pray
so that together with all mankind,
with mind and body, their entreaties may
     move you.

Through your prayer,
your anguish and merits,
may [the people] deserve to receive of the
     Lord,
born of you according to the flesh,
the benefits of grace
and the remission of sins.
Amen.

28

William Cornysh (ca. *1465–1523*)
Motet: *Ave Maria mater Dei*

Frank L. Harrison, ed., *The Eton Choirbook: III* (London: Stainer and Bell, Ltd., 1961; Musica Britannica, XII), pp. 57–58. Reprinted by permission.

Ave Maria, mater Dei regina,   Holy Mary, God's queen mother,
caeli domina   mistress of the heavens
mundi imperatrix inferni,   empress of the lower world,
miserere mei,   have mercy on me,
et totius populi Christiani,   and on the entire Christian people,
et ne permittas nos mortaliter peccare,   and permit us not to sin mortally,
sed tuam sanctissimam voluntatem adimplere. but to abide by your most holy wish.
Amen.   Amen.

Josquin des Prez (ca. 1440–1521)
Motet: *Tu solus, qui facis mirabilia*

29

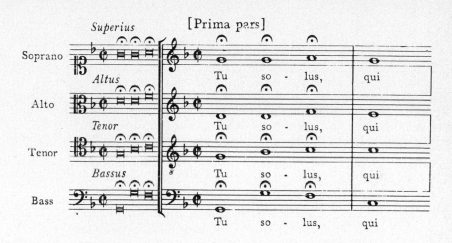

See No. 44 in this Anthology for Ockeghem's song, *D'ung aultre amer*, reworked in measures 56–72. *Motetti di passione* (Venice, 1503), ed. George Hunter in New York Pro Musica Series, no. 36 (New York/London: Associated Music Publishers, 1973, pp. 3–12. Reprinted by permission.

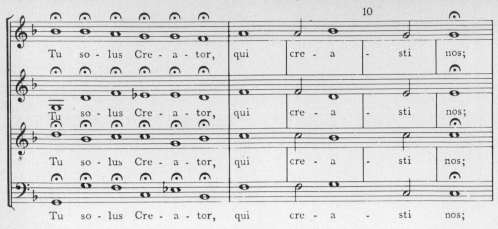

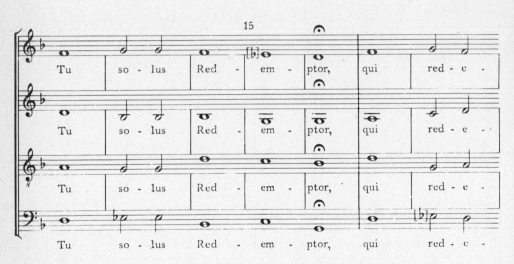

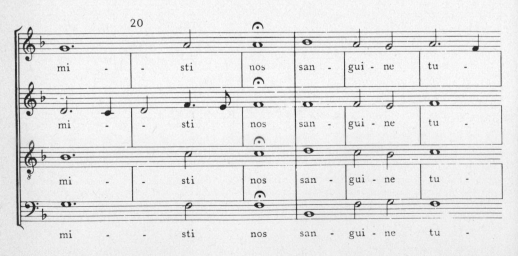

o pre - ti - o - sis - si - mo.

o pre - ti - o - sis - si - mo.

o pre - ti - o - sis - si - mo.

o pre - ti - o - sis - si - mo.

Ad te so - lum con - fu - gi - mus,

Ad te so - lum con - fu - gi - mus,

In te so - lum con - fi - di - mus, nec

In te so - lum con - fi - di - mus, nec

nec

nec

a - li - um ad - o - ra - mus,   Je - su Chri - ste.
a - li - um ad - o - ra - mus,   Je - su Chri - ste.
a - li - um ad - o - ra - mus,   Je - su Chri - ste.
a - li - um ad - o - ra - mus,   Je - su Chri - ste.

Ad   te   pre - ces_____ ef - fun - di - mus,
Ad   te   pre - ces_____ ef - fun - di - mus,

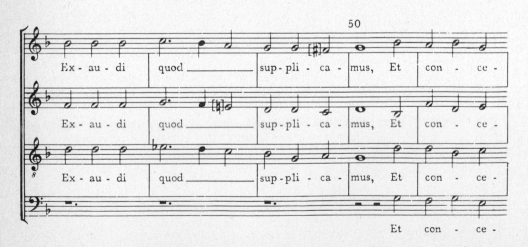

Ex - au - di   quod_____ sup - pli - ca - mus, Et   con - ce -
Ex - au - di   quod_____ sup - pli - ca - mus, Et   con - ce -
Ex - au - di   quod_____ sup - pli - ca - mus, Et   con - ce -
Et   con - ce -

de quod pe - ti - mus, Rex be - ni - gne!

de____ quod pe - ti - mus, Rex be - ni - gne!

de____ quod pe - ti - mus, Rex be - ni - gne!

de quod pe - ti - mus, Rex be - ni - gne!

[Secunda pars]

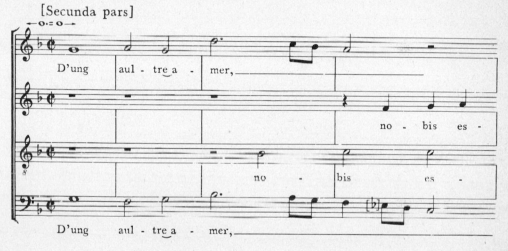

D'ung aul - tre a - mer,____

no - bis es -

no - bis es -

D'ung aul - tre a - mer,____

D'ung

set fal - la - ci - a;

set fal - la - ci - a;

D'ung

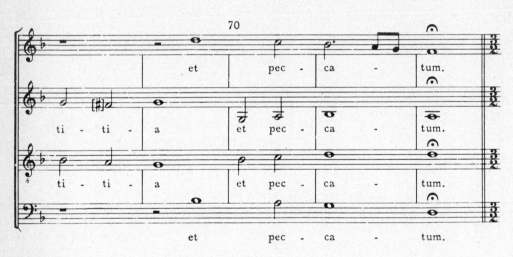

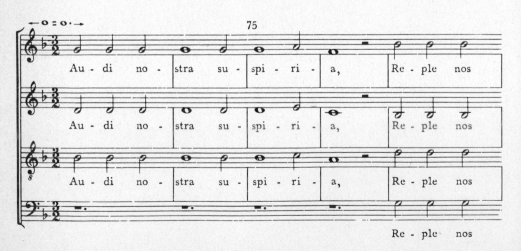

tu - a gra - ti - a, O Rex re - gnum!
tu - a gra - ti - a, O Rex re - gnum!
tu - a gra - ti - a, O Rex re - gnum!
tu - a gra - ti - a, O Rex re - gnum!

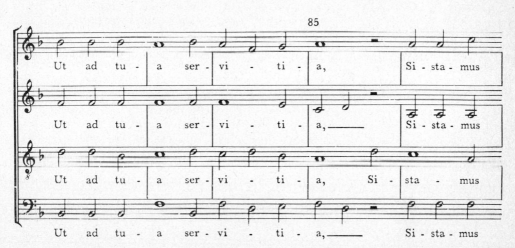

Ut ad tu - a ser - vi - ti - a, Si - sta - mus
Ut ad tu - a ser - vi - ti - a,_____ Si - sta - mus
Ut ad tu - a ser - vi - ti - a, Si - sta - mus
Ut ad tu - a ser - vi - ti - a,_____ Si - sta - mus

cum læ - ti - ti - a in æ - ter - num.
cum læ - ti - ti - a_____ in æ - ter - num.
cum læ - ti - ti - a in æ - ter - num.
cum læ - ti - ti - a_____ in æ - ter - num.

Tu solus, qui facis mirabilia;
Tu solus Creator, qui creastinos;
Tu solus Redemptor, qui redemisti nos

sanguine tuo pretiosissimo.

Ad te solum confugimus,
In te solum confidimus,
Nec alium adoramus, Jesu Christe.
Ad te preces effundimus,
Exaudi quod supplicamus,
Et concede quod petimus,
Rex benigne!

D'ung aultre amer, nobis esset fallacia;
D'ung aultre amer, magna esset stultitia et
   peccatum.
Audi nostra suspiria,
Reple nos tua gratia, O Rex regum:
Ut ad tua servitia sistamus cum laetitia in
   aeternum.

You only, who do wonders,
You, the only Creator, who created us,
You only are the Redeemer, who redeemed us
   with
Your most precious blood.

In You alone we seek refuge,
in You alone we place our trust,
and no other do we adore, Jesus Christ.
To You we offer our prayers,
hear what we beg of You,
and grant what we request,
benign King.

To love another would be deceitful:
To love another would be great folly and sin.

Hear our sighs,
fill us with your grace, O king of kings,
that we may remain in your service with joy
   forever.

Josquin des Prèz
Motet: *Dominus regnavit* Psalm 92 for Lauds

30

Tomus secundus psalmorum selectorum quatuor et quinque vocum (Nuremberg, 1539).
Josquin, *Werken,* ed. Albert J. Smijers, XVII (Amsterdam: G. Alsbach & Co., 1955), 33–40.
Used by permission of Vereniging voor Nederlandse Muziekgeschiedenis.

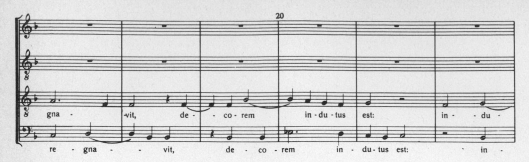

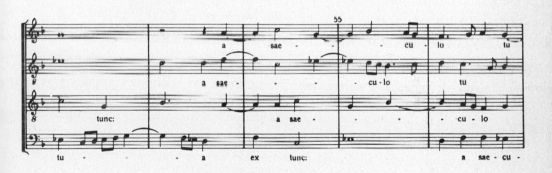

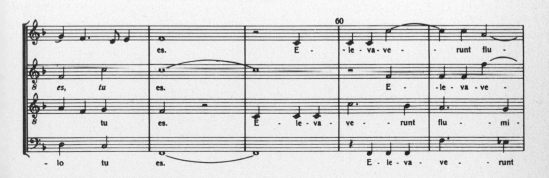

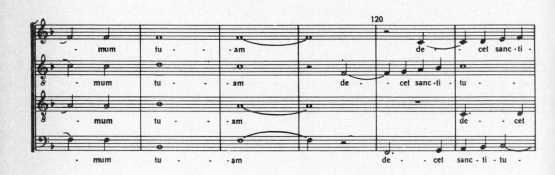

Dominus regnavit,
decorem indutus est:
indutus est Dominus fortitudinem,
et praecinxit se.
Etenim firmavit orbem terrae,
qui non commovebitur.
Parata sedes tua ex tunc:
a saeculo tu es.
Elevaverunt flumina, Domine:
elevaverunt flumina vocem suam.
Elevaverunt flumina fluctus suos,
a vocibus aquarum multarum.

Mirabiles elationes maris:
mirabilis in altis Dominus.
Testimonia tua credibilia facta sunt nimis:
domum tuam decet sanctitudo, Domine,
in longitudine dierum.
Gloria Patri et Filio,
et Spiritui Sancto.
Sicut erat in principio, et nunc, et semper,
et in saecula saeculorum, amen.

The Lord reigneth,
He is clothed with majesty;
the Lord is clothed with strength,
wherewith He hath girded himself:
the world also is established,
so that it will not be moved.
Thy throne is established of old:
Thou art from everlasting.
The floods have lifted up, O Lord,
the floods have lifted up their voice;
the floods lift up their waves,
from the sound of many waters.

As mighty as the waves of the sea
the Lord on high is mightier.
Thy testimonies are very sure:
holiness becometh thine house, O Lord
forever.
Glory be to the Father and the Son,
and the Holy Spirit.
As it was in the beginning so it ever shall be,
world without end, amen.

Adapted from the King James Version
of Psalm 93

31

Jean Mouton (*1459–1522*)
Motet: *Noe, noe*

See p. 192 for Arcadelt's Mass built upon this motet. Pierre Attaingant, ed., *Liber secundus: 24 musicales quatuor vocum Motetes* (Paris, 1534). Arcadelt, *Opera omnia,* ed. Albert Seay, I (American Institute of Musicology, 1965), 82–86. Reprinted by permission of A. Carapetyan, Director and Hänssler-Verlag, West Germany. All rights reserved. International copyright secured. Reprinted by permission.

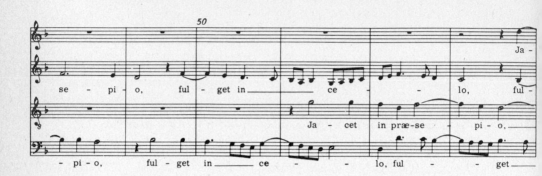

Noe, noe, psallite noe,
Jherusalem, gaude et letare,
quia hodie natus est Salvator mundi.
Jacet in praesepio, fulget in celo.
Attolite portas, principes, vestras,
et elevamini, porte eternales,
et introibit rex glorie.
Quis est iste rex glorie?
Dominus virtutum ipse est rex glorie.

Noel, noel, sing and play noel.
Jerusalem, rejoice and be glad,
for today was born the Savior of the world.
He lies in the manger, he shines in the sky.
Lift up your gates, Princes,
and be lifted up, eternal gates,
and the King of Glory will enter.
Who is this King of Glory?
The Lord of powers, he is himself the King of
    Glory.

<table>
<tr><td>

32

</td><td>

Adrian Willaert (ca. *1490–1562*)
Motet: *O crux, splendidior cunctis astris* Antiphon at First Vespers, The Finding of the Holy Cross

</td></tr>
</table>

At Magn.
Ant. 1. D

O Crux, * splendí-di- or cúnctis ástris, múndo cé-lebris, homí-ni-bus multum amá-bi- lis, sán- cti- or u-nivér-sis : quae só-la fu- ísti dígna portá- re ta-léntum múndi : dúlce lígnum, dúlces clávos, dúlci- a férens póndera : sál-va praeséntem ca-térvam, in tú- is hódi- e láudibus congre-gá-tam. *T. P.* Alle- lú- ia, alle- lú- ia. E u o u a e.

Antiphon: *LU*, 1453. Willaert, *Musica quinque vocum . . . vulgo Motecta . . . Liber primus* (Venice, 1539). *Opera omnia*, ed. Hermann Zenck, III (American Institute of Musicology, 1950), 66–72. Reprinted by permission of A. Carapetyan, Director and Hänssler-Verlag, West Germany. All rights reserved. International copyright secured. Reprinted by permission.

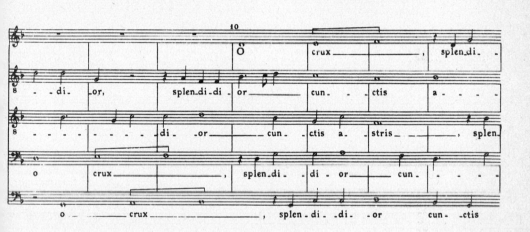

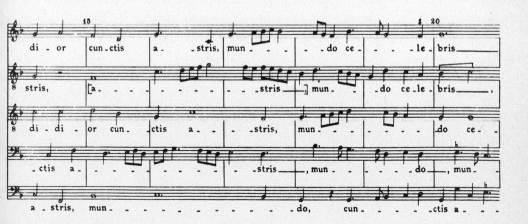

SECUNDA PARS

O crux,
splendidior cunctis astris,
mundo celebris,
hominibus multum amabilis,
sanctior universis:
quae sola fuisti digna
portare talentum mundi.
Dulce lignum,
dulces clavos,
dulcia ferens pondera:
salve praesenten capervam
in tuis hodie laudibus congregatam,
Alleluia.

O cross,
shining more brightly than all stars,
renowned throughout the world,
much beloved by mankind,
holier than all creation:
you alone were worthy
to bear the treasure of the world.
Sweet wood,
sweet nails,
bearing your sweet burden:
save this group,
gathered before you today to praise you.
Alleluia.

<table>
<tr><td>

33

</td><td>

Orlando di Lasso *(1532–94)*
Motet: *Cum essem parvulus (1579)*

</td></tr>
</table>

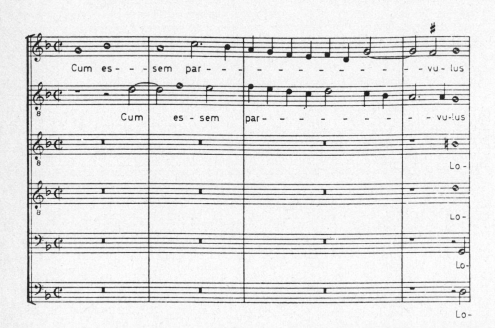

Motetta sex vocum (Munich, 1582). The motet is inscribed "August 1579" in Munich, Staatsbibliothek, Ms. 11. The text is from Epistle of St. Paul, I Corinthians 13:11. Edited in Claude V. Palisca, "Towards an Intrinsically Musical Definition of Mannerism in the Sixteenth Century," *Studi musicali,* II (1974), 332–36.

Cum essem parvulus,
loquebar ut parvulus,
sapiebam ut parvulus,
cogitabam ut parvulus;
quando autem factus sum vir,
evacuavi quae erant parvuli.
Videmus nunc per speculum
in aenigmate; tunc autem
facie ad faciem.

When I was a child,
I spoke as a child,
I understood as a child,
I thought as a child;
but when I became a man,
I put away childish things.
Now we see through a mirror
in riddles; but then
face to face.

34

William Byrd (1543–1623)
Motet: *Laudate pueri dominum*

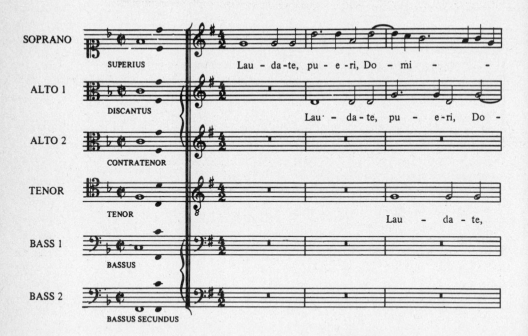

Cantiones sacrae (London, 1575). Craig Monson, ed., *The Byrd Edition*, I (London: Stainer & Bell, 1977), 82–96. Reprinted by permission.

148

Laudate, pueri, Dominum,
laudate nomen Domini:
sit nomen Domini benedictum
ex hoc nunc et usque in saeculum.

Auxilium meum a Domino,
qui fecit caelum et terram.

Bene fac, Domine,
bonis et rectis corde.

Praise, O servants of the Lord,
praise the name of the Lord.
Blessed be the name of the Lord
from this time forth and for ever.

My help comes from the Lord,
who made heaven and earth.

Do good, O Lord,
to those who are good and true.

The three sections here are drawn from three different psalms: psalm 4, verses 1 and 2; 121, verse 2; and 125, verse 4. N.B.—the text of psalm 4 is altered slightly by Byrd.

35

Guillaume Dufay (?)
Missa Caput: Agnus Dei

Ve - nit ad Pe - trum, di - xit ei Pe - trus: non la-va-bis

mi-hi pe-des in ae - ter-num. Res-pon - dens Je - sus di - xit:

si non la-ve - ro te non ha-be-bis par - tem me-cum. Do-mi - ne, non

tan-tum pe-des me-os sed et ma-nus et ca - - - - - - -

- - - - - - - - - - - put.

[Superius]   A - - - gnus de - -

Contra   A - - - gnus de - -

Tenor

Tenor 2us.

The attribution to Dufay has been contested. Alejandro Enrique Planchart, ed., *Missae Caput,* Collegium Musicum, No. 5 (New Haven: Yale University, 1964), pp. 44–52. Antiphon, *Venit ad Petrum,* for Maundy Thursday, according to Sarum rite from *ibid.,* p. viii, the source for which is British Library, MS Harley 2942, fols. 48r–48v.

For a translation of the text see p. 15.

Johannes Ockeghem (ca. *1420–97*)
Missa Caput: Agnus Dei

36

Alejandro Enrique Planchart, ed., *Missae Caput* (see note to No. 35), pp. 90–97.

Jacob Obrecht (ca. *1450/51–1505*)
Missa Caput: Agnus Dei

37

Alejandro Planchart, ed., *Missae Caput* (see note to No. 35), pp. 142–53.

John Taverner (ca. *1490–1545*)
Missa Gloria tibi trinitas: Benedictus

38

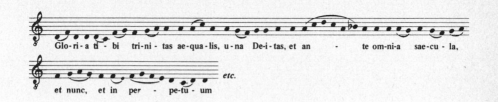

Glo-ri-a ti-bi tri-ni-tas ae-qua-lis, u-na De-i-tas, et an - te om-ni-a sae-cu-la,

et nunc, et in per - pe-tu - um *etc.*

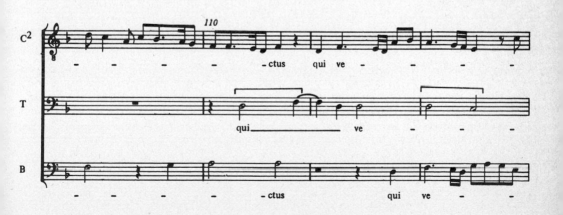

Note values quartered. See p. 288 for an "In nomine" based on the same cantus firmus. Antiphon for Second Vespers, Trinity Sunday: *Antiphonale Sarisburiense*, ed. W. H. Frere (London: Plainsong and Mediaeval Music Society, 1901–25), p. 286. Mass: *John Taverner: I. Six-Part Masses*, ed. Hugh Benham (London: Stainer and Bell, 1978), pp. 55–60. Reprinted by permission.

For a translation of the text see p. 15.

39 · Jacob Arcadelt (ca. *1505–68*)
Missa Noe noe: Kyrie and *Gloria*

Values halved. See p. 128, Mouton's motet, *Noe, noe,* upon which this Mass is based. *Missae tres Jacobo Arcadelt* (Paris, 1557). Albert Seay, ed., Arcadelt, *Opera omnia,* I (American Institute of Musicology, 1965), 1–8. Reprinted by permission of A. Carapetyan, Director and Hänssler-Verlag, West Germany. All rights reserved. International copyright secured. Reprinted by permission.

Et in terra pax hominibus bonae voluntatis.	And on earth peace to men of good will.
Laudamus te. Benedicimus te. Adoramus te. Glorificamus te.	We praise thee, we bless thee, we adore thee, we glorify thee.
Gratias agimus tibi propter magnam gloriam tuam.	We give thee thanks for thy great glory.
Domine Deus, Rex caelestis,	O Lord God, King of heaven,
Deus Pater omnipotens.	God the Father almighty.
Domine Fili unigenite Jesu Christe.	O Lord, the only begotten Son, Jesus Christ
Domine Deus, Agnus Dei, Filius Patris.	O Lord God, Lamb of God, Son of the Father.
Qui tollis peccata mundi,	Thou who takest away the sins of the world,
miserere nobis.	have mercy on us.
Qui tollis peccata mundi,	Thou who takest away the sins of the world,
suscipe deprecationem nostram.	receive our prayer.
Qui sedes ad dexteram Patris,	Thou who sittest at the right hand of the Father,
miserere nobis.	have mercy on us.
Quoniam tu solus sanctus.	For thou only art holy,
Tu solus Dominus.	Thou only art Lord.
Tu solus Altissimus, Jesu Christe.	Thou only art most high, O Jesus Christ,
Cum Sancto Spiritu,	With the Holy Ghost,
In Gloria Dei Patris. Amen.	In the glory of God the Father. Amen.

For a translation of the *Kyrie,* see p. 12.

40 Giovanni da Palestrina (1525/26–94)
Pope Marcellus Mass: Credo

Missarum Liber secundus (Rome, 1567). *Opere complete di Giovanni Pierluigi da Palestrina*, ed. Raffaele Casimiri (Rome: Edizione Fratelli-Scalera), IV (1939), 177–87.

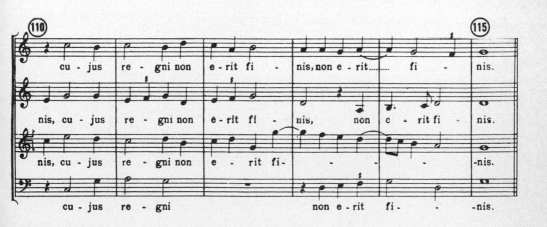

For a translation of the text, see p. 14.

Guillaume Dufay
Ballade: *Resvellies vous et faites chiere lye* (1423)

41

Opera omnia, ed. Heinrich Besseler, VI (American Institute of Musicology, 1964), pp. 25–26. Reprinted by permission of A. Carapetyan, Director and Hänssler-Verlag, West Germany. All rights reserved. International copyright secured. Reprinted by permission.

Resvellies vous et faites chiere lye
Tout amoureux qui gentilesse ames
Esbates vous, fuyes merancolye,
De bien servir point ne soyes hodés
Car au jour d'ui sera li espousés,
Par grant honneur et noble seignourie;
Ce vous convient ung chascum faire feste,
Pour bien grignier la belle compagnye;
Charle gentil, c'on dit de Maleteste.

Il a dame belle et bonne choysie,
Dont il sera grandement honnourés;
Car elle vient de tres noble lignie
Et de barons qui sont mult renommés.
Son propre nom est Victoire clamés;
De la colonne vient sa progenie.
C'est bien rayson qu'a vascule requeste
De cette dame mainne bonne vie.
Charle gentil, c'on dit de Maleteste.

Awake and be merry,
lovers all who love gentleness;
frolic and flee melancholy.
Tire not of serving yourself well,
for today will be the nuptials,
with great honor and noble lordship,
and it behooves you, everyone, to celebrate
and join the happy company.
Noble *Charles,* who is named *Malatesta.*

He has chosen a lady, fair and good,
by whom he will be greatly honored,
for she comes from a very noble lineage
of barons who are much renowned.
Her name is *Victoria,*
and she descends from the *Collonas.*
It is right, therefore, that his appeal be heard
to live honestly with this lady.
Noble *Charles,* who is named *Malatesta.*

Guillaume Dufay
Rondeau: *Adieu ces bons vins de Lannoys* (1426)

42

Contratenor

Tenor

Opera omnia, ed. Heinrich Besseler, VI (American Institute of Musicology, 1964), 50. Reprinted by permission of A. Carapetyan, Director and Hänssler-Verlag, West Germany. All rights reserved. International copyright secured. Reprinted by permission.

Adieu ces bons vins de Lannoys,   Farewell, these good wines of Lannoy.
Adieu dames, adieu borgois,   Farewell, ladies, farewell townsfolk.
Adieu celle que tant amoye,   Farewell to her whom I loved so well.
Adieu toute playsante joye   Farewell all pleasurable joy.
Adieu tous compaignons galois.   Farewell all my Welsh companions.

Je m'en vois tout arquant des nois,   I find myself searching for nuts,
Car je ne truis feves ne pois,   because I cannot find beans or peas,
Dont bien souvent [. . .]-ier mennoye.   which very often makes me annoyed.

Adieu ces bons vins de Lannoys,   Farewell, these good wines of Lannoy.
Adieu dames, adieu borgois,   Farewell ladies, farewell townsfolk.
Adieu celle que tant amoye.   Farewell to her whom I loved so well.

De moy seres, par plusieurs fois   By me you will be often
Regretés par dedans les bois,   missed, deep in the woods
Ou il n'y a sentier ne voye;   where there is no path or way;
Puis ne scaray que faire doye,   then I shall not know what I should do
Se je ne crie a haute vois.   unless I shout in a loud voice.
Adieu ces bons vins de Lannoys, etc.   Farewell, these good wines of Lannoy.

Antoine Busnois (d. *1492*)
Bergerette: *A une damme j'ay fait veu*

43

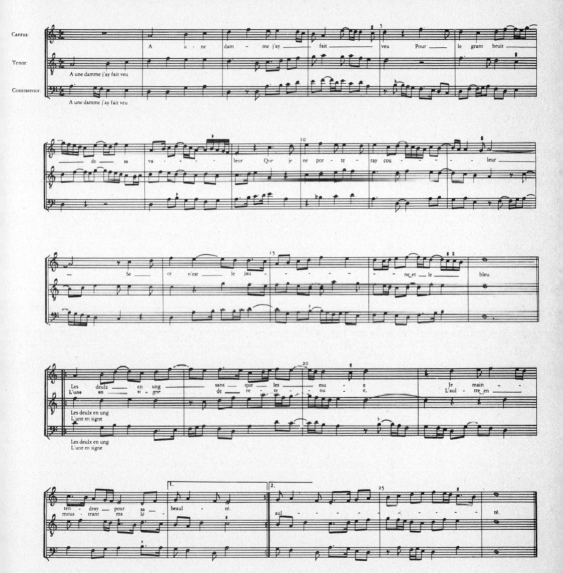

Cantus:

Tenor:

Contratenor:

A une damme j'ay fait veu

A une damme j'ay fait veu

Leeman Perkins and Howard Garey, eds., *The Mellon Chansonnier* (New Haven: Yale University Press, © 1979), I, 47, 49. Reprinted by permission.

A une damme j'ay fait veu
Pour le grant bruit de sa valeur
Que je ne porteray couleur
Se ce n'est le jaune et le bleu.

Les deulz en ung sans que les mue
Je maintendray pour sa beaulté.
L'une en signe de retenue,
L'aultre en moustrant ma léaulté.

Car au fort quant il sera sceu
Que d'elle soye serviteur,
Oncques ne m'avint tel honneur
Sans saillir l'escu tant soit peu.

To a lady I made a vow,
because of reports of her valor,
that I would not wear any color
unless it is yellow and blue.

These two in one, without changing them,
I shall retain, for her beauty.
one a sign of respect,
the other showing my fidelity.

For, indeed, when it is known
that I am her servant,
no one will ever snatch this honor from me
without sullying his shield, if only a bit.

Johannes Ockeghem
Chanson: *D'ung aultre amer mon cueur s'abesseroit*

44

See Josquin's motet, *Tu solus*, p. 111, which is partly based on this song.   Albert Smijers, ed., *Von Ockeghem tot Sweelinck* (Amsterdam: G. Alsbach & Co., 1952), II, 12. Used by permission of Vereniging voor Nederlandse Muziekgeschiedenis.

D'ung aultre amer mon cueur s'abesseroit,
Il ne fault pas penser que je l'estrange,

Ne que pour rien de ce propos me change.

Car mon honneur en appetisseroit.

Je l'aime tant que jamais ne seroit
Possible a moy d'en consentir l'echange.
D'ung aultre amer . . . (etc.)

La mort, par Dieu, avant me defferoit,
Qu'en mon vivant j'acointasse ung estrange.

Ne cuide nul qu'a cela je me renge,
Ma loyaulté trop fort se mesferoit.
D'ung aultre amer . . . (etc.)

To love another my heart would be debased.
It should not be thought that I estrange myself
    from him,
or that anything would bend me from this re-
    solve,
because my honor would be in jeopardy.

I love him so much that never would it be
possible for me to consent to an exchange.
To love another . . . (etc.)

Death, by God, would sooner unlock me
than that in my lifetime I should know a
    stranger.
Think not that I would adapt myself to this.
My fidelity would be too much damaged.
To love another . . . (etc.)

Josquin des Prez
Mille regretz

45

a) *Vocal chanson in four parts*

First published in a lute arrangement by Hans Newsidler, *Ein New geordnet Künstlich Lautenbuch* (Nuremberg, 1536). Reprinted by permission of the publishers from *The Chanson and Madrigal*, edited by James Haar. Cambridge, Mass.: Harvard University Press, © 1968 by the President and Fellows of Harvard College.

ner, brief mes jours def - fi - - ner.

ner, brief mes jours def - fi - - ner.

ner, brief mes jours def - fi - - ner.

ner, brief mes jours def - fi - - ner.

Mille regretz de vous habandonner
Et d'eslonger vostre fache amoureuse,
Jay si grand ducil et paine douloureuse,

Quon me verra brief mes jours definer.

A thousand regrets at deserting you
and leaving behind your loving face,
I feel so much sadness and such painful distress,
that it seems to me my days will soon dwindle away.

b) *Arrangement for vihuela by Luys de Narváez (after 1500?–after 1555?)*

Narváez, *Los seys libros del Delphin de música de cifras para vihuela* (Valladolid, 1538). In this source the song is named "La cancion del Emperador," and may have been among "aucunes chanssons nouvelles" delivered by Josquin to Charles V in September 1520. See *MGG*, vii, 197. Edited by Geneviève Thibault in "Instrumental Transcriptions of Josquin's French Chansons," in *Josquin des Prez*, ed. Edward E. Lowinsky (London: Oxford University Press, 1976), pp. 464–66.

46

Lied: *Nu bitten wir den heil' gen Geist*

Nu bit - ten wir den heil'- gen geist umb den rech - ten glau - ben al - ler - meist, daß er uns be - hü - te an un - serm en - de, so wir heim - farn aus die - sem e - len - de. Ky - ri - e

Glogauer Liederbuch, Berlin, Deutsche Staatsbibliothek, MS 40098 Z. 98. Reprinted by permission of Bärenreiter-Verlag, Kassel, Basel, Tours, London, from *Das Erbe deutscher Musik,* IV, edited by H. Ringmann and J. Klapper. (Kassel, etc., 1954), 5.

Nu bitten wir den heil'gen Geist
umb den rechten Glauben allermeist,
dass er uns behüte an unserm Ende,
so wir heimfarn aus diesem Elende.
Kyrie eleison.

Now we pray to the Holy Ghost
for the true faith most of all,
that He may watch over us at our end,
when we shall go homeward from this misery.
Kyrie eleison.

47

Canto carnascialesco: *Orsu car' Signori*

Johannes Wolf, ed., *Sing- und Spielmusik aus älterer Zeit* (Leipzig: Verlag von Quelle & Meyer, 1931), pp. 49–51.

Orsu, orsu, car' Signori,	Step up, dear sirs,
Chi sue bolle vol spedire,	if you wish your bulls quickly certified.
Venga ad nui che siam scripturi.	Come to us, for we are scribes.
Sù, Signori se volete	Come up, sirs, if you wish to
Vostre bolle far spacciare.	have your bulls made ready.
Et se ad nui le manderete,	And if you consign them to us,
Novelle farem stentare.	we shall not make you wait.
Ma volemo pacto fare,	We want to come to terms,
Despacciare soct'a sopra.	and do them right, above and below.
Octo el giorno et far bona opra.	Eight a day, and good work, too,
Quanto faccia altri scripturi.	as good as other scribes.

Ogni cosa in punto et bene
Et in ordine tenemo.
Per servire chi prima vene
Nostra penna in man piglemo.
Nel calamaro la mectemo
Et cacciamo for' l'ingiostro.
Se provate el servire nostro,
Non vorrete altri scripturi.
Orsu, orsu, car' Signori,
Chi soe bolle vol spedire
Venga ad nui che siam scripturi.

Every detail will be just right
and in good order.
To serve whomever first arrives
we take pen in hand.
We dip it in the ink-well
and we press the ink out.
If you try our service,
you'll not want other scribes.
Step up, dear sirs,
if you wish your bulls quickly certified.
Come to us, for we are scribes.

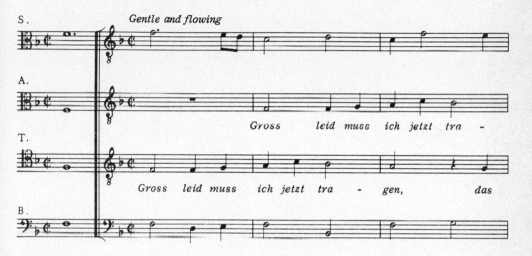

Heinrich Isaac (ca. *1450–1517*)
Innsbruck, ich muss dich lassen

48

a) Gross Leid muss ich jetzt tragen

Gentle and flowing

Gross leid muss ich jetzt tra -

Gross leid muss ich jetzt tra - gen, das

gen, das ich al - lein tu kla - gen dem

ich al - lein tu kla - gen dem lieb - sten buh - len

48a, textless in the sources, has been reconstructed from two manuscripts; the second stanza of the Lied has been set to the parts; 48b from G. Forster, *Ein ausszug guter alter und newer teutscher Liedlein* (Nuremberg, 1539).
Noah Greenberg and Paul Maynard, *An Anthology of Early Renaissance Music* (New York, 1975), pp. 181–84.

lieb - sten buh- len mein.   Ach Lieb, nun lass mich Ar -

mein.   Ach Lieb, nun lass mich Ar - men   im

men   im Her - zen dein er - bar -

Her - zen dein er - bar - men,   dass

men, dass ich   muss dan - - - - nen sein.

ich___ muss___ dan - - - - nen sein.

b) Innsbruck, ich muss dich lassen

be - kom - men, wo ich im E - - lend

be-kom - men, wo ich im E - - lend

be-kom - men, wo ich im E - - lend

be - kom - men, wo ich im E - lend, im E - lend

bin, wo ich im E - - lend bin.

bin, wo ich im E - - lend bin.

bin, wo ich im E - - lend bin.

bin, wo ich im E - - lend bin.

Innsbruck, ich muss dich lassen,
ich fahr dahin mein Strassen,
in fremde Land dahin.
Mein Freud is mir genommen,
die ich nit weiss bekommen,
wo ich im Elend bin.

Innsbruck, I must leave you
I am going on my way
into a foreign land.
My joy is taken from me,
I know not how to regain it,
while in such misery.

Gross Leid muss ich jetzt tragen,
das ich allein tu klagen
dem liebsten Buhlen mein.
Ach Lieb, nun lass mich Armen
im Herzen dein erbarmen,
dass ich muss dannen sein.

I must now endure great pain
which I confide only
to my dearest love.
O beloved, find pity
in your heart for me,
that I must part from you.

Mein Trost ob allen Weiben,
dein tu ich ewig bleiben,
stet treu, der Ehren fromm.
Nun muss dich Gott bewahren,
in aller Tugend sparen,
bis dass ich wiederkomm.

My comfort above all other women,
I shall always be yours,
forever faithful in honor true.
May the good Lord protect you
and keep you in your virtue
for me, till I return.

N. GREENBERG and P. MAYNARD

Claudin de Sermisy (ca. *1490–1562*)
Chanson: *Vivray–je tousjours en soucy*

49

Pierre Attaingnant, ed., *Chansons nouvelles* (Paris, 1527). *Opera omnia*, IV, *Chansons,* ed. Isabelle Cazeaux (American Institute of Musicology, 1974), 127–28. Reprinted by permission of A. Carapetyan, director and Hänssler-Verlag, West Germany. All rights reserved. International copyright secured. Reprinted by permission.

Vivray—je tousjours en soucy
Pour vous, ma tres loyalle amye?
Si vous n'avez de moy mercy
Je languiray toute ma vie.
Vostre beaulté m'a arresté pour son servant;
Du tres bon coeur son serviteur me vois nom-
    mant.

Shall I always be anxious
about you, my very faithful love?
If you do not have pity for me,
I shall be melancholy all my life.
Your beauty has captured me as its slave;
in good faith I call myself your servant.

Je l'ay aymée et l'aymeray
Pour le grant bien qui est en elle.
Et jamais ne l'obliray
Par quelque chose que ce soit,
Car son maintien.
Et entretien
Est si plaisant
Que langoreulx
Seroit joyeulx
Incontinent.

I have loved her and I shall love her
for the great good that is in her.
And never will I forget her
for any reason whatever,
because her bearing
and conversation
are so pleasant
that a languishing [lover]
would be happy
forthwith.

Io non com - pro più spe - ran - za Ché gli è fal - sa mercan ci - a.

A dar sol at - ten - do vi - a Quella po - ca che m'a - van - za.

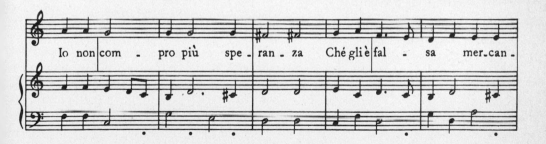

Io non com - pro più spe - ran - za Ché gli è fal - sa mer - can -

Note values halved. Notes in the lute part with dots under them are played with an upward stroke. Bars through the lute staves are original. Those between the voice part and lute accompaniment are added by the present editor to show the true metrical organization. Franciscus Bossinensis, ed., *Tenori e contrabassi intabulati col sopran in canto figurato per cantar e sonar col lauto, libro primo* (Venice, 1509). Benvenuto Disertori, ed., *Le Frottole per canto e liuto intabulate da Franciscus Bossinensis* (Milan: Ricordi, 1964), pp. 390–91. Reprinted by permission.

letterale   letterale

Io non compro più speranza	I'll buy no more hope,
Ché gli è falsa mercancia	which is fake goods;
A dar sol attendo via	I can't wait to give away
Quella poca che m'avanza.	the little that I have left.
Io non compro più speranza	I'll buy no more hope,
Ché gli è falsa mercancia.	which is fake goods.

Cara un tempo la comprai,	Once I bought it dear;
Hor la vendo a bon mercato	now I sell it cheap;
E consiglio ben che mai	and I would advise that never
Non ne compri un sventurato	should the wretched buy it;
Ma più presto nel suo stato	rather let them in their condition
Se ne resti con costanza.	remain in constancy.
Io non . . .	I'll buy . . .

El sperare è come el sogno	To hope is like a dream
Che per più riesce in nulla,	that mostly results in nothing,
El sperar è proprio il bisogno	and hoping is the craving need
De chi al vento si trastulla,	of him who plays with the wind.
El sperare sovente anulla	Hoping often annihilates
Chi continua la sua danza.	the one who continues its dance.
Io non . . .	I'll buy . . .

Jacob Arcadelt
Madrigal: *Ahime, dov' è 'l bel viso*

51

Values halved. *Il primo libro di Madrigali d'Archadelt a quatro con nuova gionta impressi* (Venice, 1539; first edition lost but probably from 1538). Albert Seay, ed., Arcadelt, *Opera omnia*, II (American Institute of Musicology, 1970), 1–3. Reprinted by permission of A. Carapetyan, Director and Hänssler-Verlag, West Germany. All rights reserved. International copyright secured. Reprinted by permission.

Ahime, dov'è 'l bel viso,
In cui solea tener nid' amore,
E dove ripost'era ogni mia speme,
Ch'ornav'il mondo di splendore,
Il mio caro thesoro, il sommo bene?
Oime, chi me 'l ritien', chi me lo cela?

O fortuna, o mort'ingorda,
Cicca spietat'e sorda,
Chi m'ha tolto 'l mio cor, chi me l'asconde?

Dov'è 'l ben mio che più non mi risponde?

Alas, where is the pretty face
in which love used to nest
and where rested my every hope,
adorning the world with splendor
My dear treasure, the highest good?
Alas, who keeps it from me, who hides it from me?

O luck, o greedy death,
blind, merciless and dumb.
Who has snatched away my heart, who hides it from me?

Where is my darling who answers me no more?

52

Adrian Willaert
Madrigal: *Aspro core e selvaggio e cruda voglia*

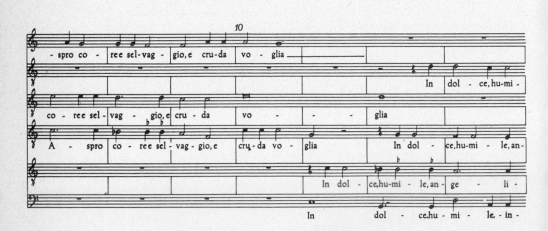

Willaert, *Musica nova* (Venice, 1559). This madrigal was probably composed in the mid-1540s. *Opera omnia*, ed. Hermann Zenck and Walter Gerstenberg, XIII (American Institute of Musicology, 1966), 54–60. Reprinted by permission of A. Carapetyan, Director and Hänssler-Verlag, West Germany. All rights reserved. International copyright secured. Reprinted by permission.

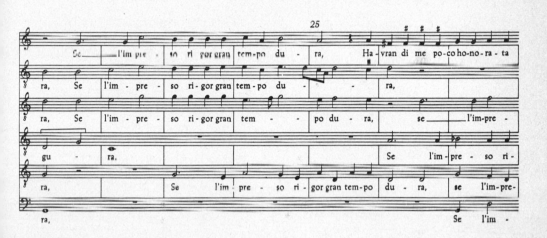

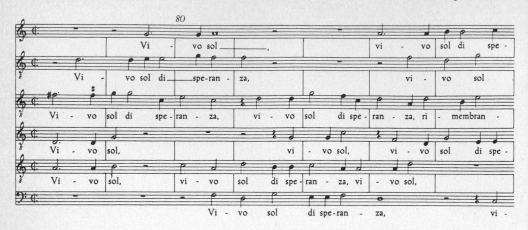

Aspro core e selvaggio, e cruda voglia
In dolce, umile, angelica figura,
Se l'impreso rigor gran tempo dura,
Avran di me poco honorata spoglia,
Che, quando nasce e mor fior, erba e foglia,

Quando è 'l dí chiaro e quando è notte oscura,

Piango ad ogni or. Ben ho di mia ventura,
Di madonna e d'Amore onde mi doglia.
Vivo sol di speranza, rimenbrando
Che poco umor già per continua prova
Consumar vidi marmi e pietre salde.

Non è sí duro cor che, lagrimando,
Pregando, amando, talhor non si smova,
Né sí freddo voler, che non si scalde.

FRANCESCO PETRARCA (1304–74)

Harsh heart and savage, and a cruel will
in a sweet, humble, angelic face,
if this adopted severity persist for long,
they will get from me spoils of little honor;
for when flower, grass, and leaf are born and
    die,
when it is shining day and when it is dark
    night,
I weep at every season. Well may I grieve,
for my luck, my lady and my love.
I live by hope alone, remembering
that by continuous drops
I have seen little liquid consume marble and
    solid stones.
There is no heart so hard that weeping,
begging, loving sooner or later does not move,
nor so cold a resolve that it cannot be warmed.

<table>
<tr><td>53</td><td>**Cipriano de Rore** *(1516–65)*
Madrigal: *Datemi pace, o duri miei*
pensieri</td></tr>
</table>

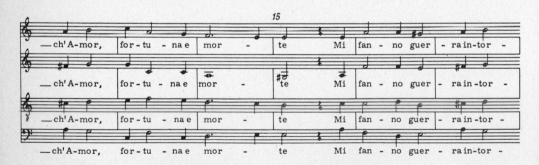

Di Cipriano de Rore il secondo libro de madregali a quattro voci (Venice, 1557). *Opera omnia,* ed. Bernhard Meier, IV (American Institute of Musicology, 1969), 73–75. Reprinted by permission of A. Carapetyan, Director and Hänssler-Verlag, West Germany. All rights reserved. International copyright secured. Reprinted by permission.

In tei se-cre-ti suoi mes-sag-gi A-mo - re, In te spie-
In tei se-cre-ti suoi mes-sag-gi A-mo - re, In te spie-
gie - ri. In tei se-cre-ti suoi mes-sag-gi A-mo - re, In te spie-
mi-ci sì pron-ti e leg-gie - ri.   In te spie-ga

ga for-tu - na o-gni sua pom - pa E mor - te la me-
ga for-tu - na o-gni sua pom - pa E mor-te la me-mo -
- ga for-tu - na o-gni sua pom - pa E mor-te la me-mo - ria
for-tu - na o-gni sua pom - pa E mor - te la me-mo -

mo-ria di quel col - po Che l'a-van - zo di me con-vien che rom - pa;
ria di quel col - po Che l'a-van - zo di me con-vien che rom - pa;
di quel col - po Che l'a-van - zo di me con-vien che rom - pa;
ria di quel col - po Che l'a-van - zo di me con-vien che rom - pa;

In tei va - ghi pen-sier s'ar - man d'er-ro - re: Per-chè
In tei va - ghi pen-sier s'ar - man d'er-ro - re: Per-chè
In tei va - ghi pen-sier s'ar - man d'er-ro - re: Per-chè
In tei va - ghi pen-sier s'ar - man d'er-ro - re: Per-chè

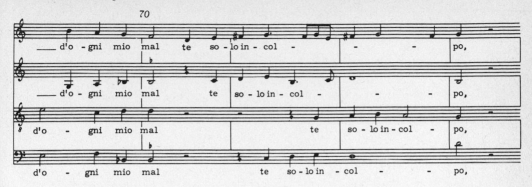

Datemi pace, o duri miei pensieri:
Non basta ben ch'Amor Fortuna e Morte
Mi fanno guerra intorno, e 'n su le porte,
Senza trovarmi dentro altri guerreri?
E tu, mio cor, ancor se' pur qual eri?
Disleal a me sol; che fere scorte

Vai ricettando e se' fatto consorte
De' miei nemici sì pronti e leggieri.
In te i secreti suoi messaggi, Amore,
In te spiega Fortuna ogni sua pompa,
E Morte la memoria di quel colpo
Che l'avanzo di me convèn che rompa;

In te i vaghi pensier s'arman d'errore:

Per che d'ogni mio mal te solo incolpo.

Oh, give me peace, my jarring thoughts.
Is it not enough that Love, Fate, and Death
wage war all about me and at my very gates,
without finding other enemies within?
And you, my heart, are you still as you were?
Disloyal to me alone: for you harbor fierce
    spies
and have allied yourself
with my enemies, bold and brisk as they are.
In you Love reveals his secret messages,
in you Fate boasts all her triumphs,
and Death [awakens] the memory of that blow
which must surely destroy all that remains of
    me;
In you gentle thoughts arm themselves with
    falsity:
Wherefore I charge you alone guilty of all my
    ills.

F. PETRARCA

Madrigali a cinque voci, Libro quinto (Milan, 1572). *Opera omnia,* ed. Henry W. Kaufmann (American Institute of Musicology, 1963), pp. 96–101. Reprinted by permission of A. Carapetyan, Director. and Hänssler-Verlag, West Germany.
All rights reserved. International copyright secured. Reprinted by permission.

L'aura che 'l verde lauro et l'aureo crine
Soavemente sospirando move,
Fa con sue viste leggiadrette e nove
L'anime da' lor corpi pellegrine.

Candida rosa nata in dure spine
Quando fia chi sua pari al mondo trove?
Gloria di nostra etate! O vivo Giove,
Manda, prego, il mio in prima che 'l suo fine:
Si ch'io non veggia il gran publico danno
E 'l mondo remaner senza 'l suo sole,
Né gli occhi miei che luce altra non hanno,
Né l'anima, che pensar d'altro non vole,
Né l'orecchie, ch'udir altro non sanno,
Senza l'honeste sue dolci parole.

The breeze which softly sighing moves the
        green laurel and the golden hair,
with their aspects graceful and new
makes souls set forth like pilgrims from their
        bodies.

Spotless rose, born among sharp thorns,
when will her equal be found on earth?
Glory of our age! O living Jupiter,
send, I beg, mine before her end:
so that I may not see the great public loss,
the world left without its sun,
nor my eyes, that have no other light,
nor my mind, which will think of nothing else,
nor my ears, which cannot hear anything else,
[left] without her chaste sweet words.

F. PETRARCA

55

Carlo Gesualdo (ca. *1560–1613*)
Madrigal: *"Io parto" e non più dissi*

Gesualdo, *Madrigali a cinque voci; Libro sesto* (Gesualdo, 1611). *Sämtliche Madrigale für fünf Stimmen*, ed., Wilhelm Weismann, I, 29–32. © 1957 by Ugrino Verlag, Hamburg. Assigned to VEB Deutscher Verlag für Musik, Leipzig; Alexander Broude, Inc., Sole Agent. Reprinted by permission.

"Io parto" e non più dissi che il dolore
Privò di vita il core.
Allor proruppe in pianto e dissi Clori
Con interroti omèi:
"Dunque a i dolori io resto. Ah, non fia mai

Ch'io non languisca in dolorosi lai."
Morto fui, vivo son che i spirti spenti

tornaro in vita a sì pietosi accenti.

"I depart" and said no more, for grief
robbed the heart of life.
Then he broke out in tears, and Clori said,
with interrupted cries of "Alas":
"Therefore, with my pains I remain. Ah, may
I never
cease to languish in painful lays."
Dead I was, now am I alive, for the dead
spirits
return to life at the sound of such pitiable accents.

Thomas Weelkes (ca. 1575–1623)
Madrigal: *O Care, thou wilt despatch me*

56

Weelkes, *Madrigals of 5 and 6 parts* (London, 1600). Edmund Fellowes, ed., *The English Madrigalists* (London: Stainer and Bell, 1968), XI, 19–29. Reprinted by permission.

John Wilbye *(1574–1638)*
Madrigal: *Stay Corydon thou swain*

57

The Second Set of Madrigales to 3, 4, 5, and 6 parts apt for Voyals and Voyces (London, 1609). E. H. Fellowes, ed., *The English Madrigalists*, revised by Thurston Dart, VII (London: Stainer and Bell, 1966), 214–23. Reprinted by permission.

58

Pierre Attaingnant (d. *1552*)*
Danseries a 4 Parties, Second Livre

a) Basse danse (No. 1)

*Editor of the collection. Note values reduced by half. Barlines through the entire brace mark the *quaternions* of the choreography; triple-time measures are set off by barlines through the staff; after every seventh minim of a *quaternion* a broken line appears. *Danseries a 4 parties, Second livre* (Paris, 1547), ed. Raymond Meylan (Paris: Heugel & Cie., c1969), pp. 1, 38–39. Used by permission of the Publisher, Theodore Presser Company, sole representative U.S.A.

b) Branle gay *Que je chatoulle ta fossette* (No. 36)

Robert Morton (ca. *1440–75*)
Chanson: *L'omme armé* for instruments

59

Jeanne Marix, *Les musiciens de la cour de Bourgogne au xvie siècle* (Paris: Éditions de L'Oiseau-lyre, 1937), p. 96.
Reprinted by permission.

60

Luis Milan (ca. *1500*–after *1561*)
Fantasia XI for vihuela

Moderato e Rubato

Values halved. Milan, *Libro de musica de vihuela de mano, intitulado El Maestro,* ed. Charles Jacobs (University Park and London: The Pennsylvania State University Press, 1971), pp. 59–62. Reprinted by permission.

61

Christopher Tye (ca. *1500*–ca. *1572*)
In nomine "Crye"

See no. 38 for the cantus firmus on which this is based. Christopher Tye, *The Instrumental Music*, ed. Robert W. Weidner (New Haven: A–R Editions, 1967), pp. 34–38. Reprinted by permission.

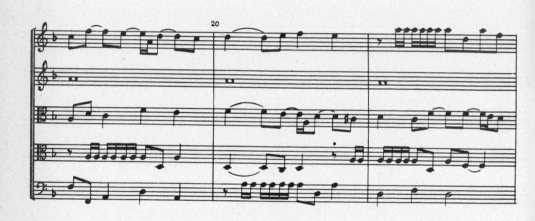

*The rest is reduced by two-thirds.

**minim (quarter note in transcription) in the MS

*d in the MS

°°G in the MS

Reprinted by permission of the publishers from *The Complete Works of Anthony Holborne*, Vol. II: *Music for Cittern*, edited by Mazakata Kanazawa (Harvard Publications in Music, 5). Cambridge, Mass.: Harvard University Press, © 1973 by the President and Fellows of Harvard College.

63   Giulio Caccini (ca. *1550–1618*)
Madrigal: *Perfidissimo volto*

Le nuove musiche (Florence, 1602). H. Wiley Hitchcock, editor, *Giulio Caccini, Le nuove musiche* (Madison: A–R Editions, Inc., 1970), p. 77–80.

spi- ra L'ab- ban- do- na- to___ co- re! O

___ vol-to trop-po va- go e trop- - po ri- o, Per-chè se per-dia-mo-re Non

per-di an-cor' va- ghez- za? O non hai pa- ri, o non___ hai___

pa- ri al-la bel- tà fer- mez- za? O___ vol- to trop- po

va-go e trop- - po ri- o, Per-chè se per-dia-mo-re Non per- di an-cor' va-

Perfidissimo volto,
Ben l'usata bellezza in te si vede
Ma non l'usata fede.
Già mi parevi dir: Quest'amorose
Luci che dolcemente
Rivolgo a te, sì bell'e sì pietose

Prima vedrai tu spente,
Che sia spento il desio ch'a te le gira.
Ahi, che spento è 'l desio,
Ma non è spento quel per cui sospira
L'abbandonato core!
O volto troppo vago e troppo rio,
Perchè se perdi amore
Non perdi ancor' vaghezza
O non hai pari alla belta fermezza?

GIOVANNI BATTISTA GUARINI (1538–1612)

O, most perfidious face,
true, the usual beauty in you is seen,
but not the usual fidelity.
Once you seemed to say: "These amorous
eyes that sweetly
I turn towards you, so beautiful and so compassionate —
first you will see these lights extinguished
before is spent the desire that they convey."
Alas, now spent is that desire,
but not spent is that for which sighs
the abandoned heart!
O face too lovely and too cruel,
why when you lose love,
do you not lose also loveliness,
and why do you not match beauty with con-
stancy?

64

Claudio Monteverdi *(1567–1643)*
Madrigal: *Cruda Amarilli*

Monteverdi, *Il quinto libro de madrigali a cinque voci* (Venice, 1606). *Tutte le opere di Claudio Monteverdi,* edited by G. Francesco Malipiero (Asolo, 1926; reprinted Vienna: Universal Edition), Vol. V, pp. 1–4. Used by permission of European American Music Distributors Corp. Sole U.S. Agent for Universal Edition, Vienna.

Cruda Amarilli che col nome ancora
D'amar, ahi lasso, amaramente insegni.
Amarilli del candido ligustro,
Più candida e più bella,
Ma dell'aspido sordo
E più sorda e più fera e più fugace.
Poi che col dir t'offendo
I mi morò tacendo.

                              G. B. GUARINI

Cruel Amaryllis, who with your name
to love, alas, bitterly you teach.
Amaryllis, more than the white privet
pure, and more beautiful,
but deafer than the asp,
and fiercer and more elusive.
Since telling I offend you,
I shall die in silence.

Prima parte

Ohi _ _ _ _ mè dov'è il mio ben

Ohi _ _ _ _ mè dov'è il mio ben dov'è il mio ben

(Andante moderato)

do _ v'è il mio co _ re do _ v'è il mio co _ _

do _ v'è il mio co _ re do _ v'è il mio co _ _ _ _

Concerto, Settimo libro de madrigali a 1. 2. 3. 4. & 6. voci, con altri generi de canti (Venice, 1619). *Tutte le opere di Claudio Monteverdi,* edited by G. Francesco Malipiero (Asolo, 1926; reprinted Vienna: Universal Edition), Vol. VII, pp. 152–59. Used by permission of European American Music Distributors Corp. Sole U.S. Agent for Universal Edition, Vienna.

Seconda parte

_gion di tan __ te di tan __ te di tan __ te do ___ glie.

_gion di tan ____ te di tan ____ te do _____ glie.

Terza parte

Dun_que ha po_tuto in me   Dun_que ha po_tuto in

Dun_que ha po_tuto in me Dun_que ha po_tuto in

(Andante)

me   in me   più che'l mio amo_re   in me   più che'l mio A_

me   più che'l mio amo_re   in me   più che'l mio A mo _____

Quarta e ultima parte

(Andante)

Ohimè dov'è il mio ben, dov'è il mio core?
Chi m'asconde il mio ben e chi m'el toglie?

Dunque ha potuto sol desio d'honore
Darmi fera cagion di tante doglie.

Dunque ha potuto in me più che'l mio amore
Ambizios'e troppo lievi voglie.
Ahi sciocco mondo e cieco, ahi cruda sorte
Che ministro mi fai della mia morte.

BERNARDO TASSO (1493–1569)

Alas, where is my love, where is my heart?
Who conceals my treasure and who takes it
away?

Thus desire for honor alone was capable
of giving me strong grounds for so many
griefs.

Thus more power than my love had my
ambitious and too trifling aspirations.
Ah, stupid world, and blind; ah, cruel fate!
You make me executioner of my own death.

<table>
<tr><td>

66

</td><td>

John Dowland *(1562–1626)*
Air: *Flow my tears*

</td></tr>
</table>

See Dowland's lute arrangement and the variations upon it by Byrd, Farnaby and Sweelinck in No. 98. *Second Booke of Songes* (London, 1600). *The English Lute Songs,* Series I, edited by Edmund H. Fellowes, revised by Thurston Dart, V–VI (London: Stainer & Bell, 1969), 4–6. Reprinted by permission.

Hark! you sha - dows that in dark - - ness

dwell, Learn to con-temn light. Hap - py, hap - py they

that in hell Feel not the world's de - - spite.

Never may my woes be relieved,
    Since pity is fled;
And tears and sighs and groans my weary days
    Of all joys have deprived.

From the highest spire of contentment
    My fortune is thrown;
And fear and grief and pain for my deserts
    Are my hopes, since hope is gone.

Hark! you shadows that in darkness dwell,
    Learn to contemn light.
Happy, happy they that in hell
    Feel not the world's despite.

67 Emilio de' Cavalieri *(1550–1602)*
Madrigal: *Dalle più alte sfere,*
Intermedio I, *1589*

(a) Sans barres de mesure. (b) En partition, avec barres de mesure.

This madrigal has also been attributed to Antonio Archilei. *Intermedii et concerti, fatti per la commedia rappresentata in Firenze nelle nozze del Serenissimo Don Ferdinando Medici, e Madama Christiana di Loreno, Gran Duchi di Toscana* (Venice, 1951). Edited by D. P. Walker, *Musique des intermèdes de "La Pellegrina"* (Paris: Éditions du Centre national de la recherche scientifique, 1963), pp. 2–8.

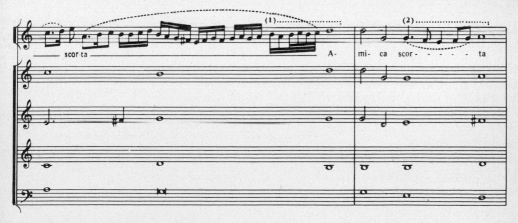

l'a - - li batten - - do   l'a - - - - - - - li   L'al - - ta fiam - ma L'al - ta

25

fiam - ma N'ap - - por - - - - ta N'ap-por - - - - - - - - - - - - - - ta

Che mai si no - - bil _____ cop - - pia'l sol _____ non _____

(1)

Dalle più alte sfere
Di celesti sirene amica scorta
Son l'armonia ch'a voi vengo mortali,
Poscia, che fino al ciel battendo l'ali
L'alta fiama n'apporta,
Che mai si nobil coppia 'l sol non vide
Qual voi nova Minerva e fort'Alcide.

GIOVANNI DE' BARDI (1534–1612)

From the highest spheres
of the heavenly sirens, a friendly escort,
I am Harmony, who comes to you mortals,
since even high in the sky, beating its wings,
lofty fame brought news
that never so noble a couple the sun did see
as you, new Minerva and brave Hercules.

68

Jacopo Peri (1561–1633)
Le musiche sopra l'Euridice

a) *Prologo, La Tragedia,* Io, che d'alti sospir vaga e di pianti

b) *Tirsi,* Nel pur ardor della più bella stella

Note values reduced by half. Original barring retained. Time signatures added by editor are in brackets; editorial accidentals are above staff. In the Prologue, the composer intended that rhythmic adjustments be made in the strophes. Peri, *Le musiche sopra l'Euridice* (Florence, 1601), pp. 2, 11–12, 14–17.

c) *Dafne,* Per quel vago boschetto
   Arcetro, Che narri, ohimè
   Orfeo, Non piango e non sospiro

tol - to o - hi - mè! ____ do - ve sei gi - ta?

To - sto ve - drai __ ch'in va - no Non chia - ma - sti mo - ren - do il _ tuo con - sor - te. Non

son, non son lon - ta - no: Io ven - go o ca - ra vi - ta, o ca - ra mor - te

PROLOGUE: TRAGEDY

Io, che d'alti sospir vaga e di pianti,	I, who with deep sighs and tears am smitten,
Spars' or di doglia, hor di minaccie il volto,	my face, covered now with grief, now with menace,
Fei negl'ampi teatri al popol folto	once in ample theatres crowded with people
Scolorir di pietà volti e sembianti.	made their faces turn pale with pity.
Non sangue sparso d'innocenti vene,	Not of blood spilled from innocent veins,
Non ciglia spente di tiranno insano,	nor of eyes put out by an insane tyrant,
Spettacolo infelice al guardo umano,	but a spectacle unhappy to the human sight,
Canto su meste e lagrimose scene.	do I sing on this sad and tearful stage.
Lungi via, lungi pur da' regi tetti	Stay far from under this royal roof,
Simulacri funesti, ombre d'affanni:	dismal images, shadows of anguish.
Ecco i mesti coturni e i foschi panni	Behold, the gloomy buskins and the dark rags
Cangio, e desto ne i cor più dolci affetti.	I transform, and awaken in the hearts sweeter affections.
Hor s'avverràche le cangiate forme	Now, if it should happen that the changed forms
Non senza alto stupor la terra ammiri,	not without great amazement the world should admire,

Tal ch'ogni alma gentil ch'Apollo inspiri
Del mio novo cammin calpesti l'orme,

so that every gentle genius that Apollo inspires
takes up the tracks, of my new path,

Vostro, Regina, fia cotanto alloro,
Qual forse anco non colse Atene, o Roma,

Yours, Queen, will be so much laurel
that perhaps not even Athens or Rome won more,

Fregio non vil su l'onorata chioma,
Fronda Febea fra due corone d'oro.

no mean ornament on the honored head,
a leafy branch of Phoebus between two crowns.

Tal per voi torno, e con sereno aspetto

Thus for you I return, and with a serene countenance

Ne' reali Imenei m'adorno anch'io,
E su corde più liete il canto mio
Tempro, al nobile cor dolce diletto.

at this royal wedding I too adorn myself,
and with happier notes my song
I temper, for the noble heart's sweet delight.

Mentre Senna real prepara intanto
Alto diadema, onde il bel crin si fregi

Meanwhile the royal Seine prepares
a lofty diadem with which the beautiful hair to crown

E i manti e' seggi de gl'antichi regi,
Del Tracio Orfeo date l'orecchie al canto.

and the cloaks and thrones of ancient kings;
to the song of the Thracian Orpheus, lend your ears.

TIRSI

Nel pur ardor della più bella stella
Aurea facella di bel foc'accendi,
E qui discendi su l'aurate piume,
Giocondo Nume, e de celeste fiamma
L'anime infiamma.

With the pure flame of the brightest star
light the golden torch with beautiful fire
and here descend on aurous wings,
o happy God, and with celestial fire
the souls inflame.

TIRSI

Lieto Imeneo d'alta dolcezza un nembo

Happy Hymen, let your shower of lofty sweetness

Trabocca in grembo a' fortunati amanti

overflow into the breasts of the fortunate lovers

E tra bei canti di soavi amori
Sveglia nei cori una dolce aura, un riso
Di Paradiso.

and, amidst pretty songs of delightful loves,
stir in their hearts a gentle breeze, a smile
of Paradise.

DAFNE

Per quel vago boschetto,
Ove, rigando i fiori,
Lento trascorre il fonte degl'allori,
Prendea dolce diletto
Con le compagne sue la bella sposa,
Chi violetta o rosa
Per far ghirland' al crine
Togliea dal prato o dall'acute spine,
E qual posand' il fianco
Su la fiorita sponda
Dolce cantava al mormorar dell 'onda;
Ma la bella Euridice

In the beautiful thicket,
where, watering the flowers,
slowly passing the fount of the laurel,
she took sweet delight
with her companions—the beautiful bride—
as some picked violets, others, roses,
to make garlands for their hair,
in the meadow or among the sharp thorns.
Another, lying on her side
on the flowered bank,
sang sweetly to the murmur of the waves.
But the lovely Eurydice

Movea danzando il piè sul verde prato

Quand'ahi ria sorte acerba,
Angue crudo e spietato
Che celato giacea tra fiori e l'erba
Punsele il piè con sì maligno dente,
Ch'impalidì repente
Come raggio di sol che nube adombri.
E dal profondo core,
Con un sospir mortale,
Si spaventoso ohimè sospinse fuore,
Che, quasi avesse l'ale,
Giunse ogni Ninfa al doloroso suono.
Et ella in abbandono
Tutta lasciossi all'or nell'altrui braccia.
Spargea il bel volto e le dorate chiome

Un sudor viè più fredd'assai che giaccio.
Indi s'udio 'l tuo nome
Tra le labbra sonar fredd'e' tremanti
E volti gl'occhi al cielo,
Scolorito il bel volto e' bei sembianti,
Restò tanta bellezza immobil gielo.

was moving, with dancing steps, her feet on
    the green grass
when—o bitter, angry fate!
a snake, cruel and merciless,
that lay hidden among flowers and grass
bit her foot with such an evil tooth
that she suddenly became pale
like a ray of sunshine that a cloud darkens.
And from the depths of her heart,
a mortal sigh,
so frightful, alas, flew forth,
almost as if it had wings;
every nymph rushed to the painful sound.
And she, fainting,
let herself fall in another's arms.
Then spread over her beautiful face and her
    golden tresses
a sweat colder by far than ice.
And then was heard your name, sounding
between her lips, cold and trembling,
and her eyes turned to heaven,
her beautiful face and mien discolored,
this great beauty was transformed to motion-
    less ice.

ARCETRO

Che narri, ohimè, che sento?
Misera Ninfa, e più misero amante,
Spettacol di miseria e di tormento!

What do you relate, alas, what do I hear?
Wretched nymph, and more unhappy lover,
spectacle of sorrow and of torment!

ORFEO

Non piango e non sospiro,
O mia cara Euridice,
Ché sospirar, ché lacrimar non posso.
Cadavero infelice,
O mio core, o mia speme, o pace, o vita!
Ohimè, chi mi t'ha tolto,
Chi mi t'ha tolto, ohimè! dove sei gita?

Tosto vedrai ch'in vano
Non chiamasti morendo il tuo consorte.
Non son, non son lontano:
Io vengo, o cara vita, o cara morte.

I do not weep, nor do I sigh,
o my dear Eurydice,
for I am unable to sigh, to weep.
Unhappy corpse,
o my heart, o my hope, o peace, o life!
Alas, who has taken you from me?
Who has taken you away, alas? Where have
    you gone?

Soon you will see then not in vain
did you, dying, call your spouse.
I am not far away:
I come, o dear life, o dear death.

OTTAVIO RINUCCINI (1562–1621)

Claudio Monteverdi
L'Orfeo, Favola in musica

69

a) *Prologo, La Musica,* Dal mio Permesso amato a voi ne vegno

Correction to the score: p. 343, m. 31, instead of C, the bass should be C-sharp, as it is in the 1609 and 1615 editions. *Tutte le opere di Claudio Monteverdi,* edited by G. Francesco Malipiero (Asola, 1926; reprinted Vienna: Universal Edition), Vol. XI, 3-18, 48-50, 59-65. Used by permission of European American Music Distributors Corp. Sole U.S. Agent for Universal Edition, Vienna.

Ritornello

(Allegro)

Io la mu_si_ca son ch'ai dol_ci ac_cen___ti so far tranquil_lo

o_gni tur_ba_to co_re et hor di no_bi_l'i_ra et hor d'a_

_mo_re pos_____s'in_fiammar le più ge_la_te men_ti.

Ritornello
(Allegro)

Io su ce te ra d'or cantan do so glio mor tal o rec chio

lu sin gar ta l'ho ra e in que sta gui sa a l'ar mo

nia so no ra de la li ra del ciel più l'al me in vo glio.

Ritornello
(Allegro)

Quin _ ci a dir _ vi d'Orfeo   de _ sio mi spro _ _ _ na,   d'Or _ feo che tras _ se

al suo can _ tar   le fe _ re   e ser _ vo fe' l'In _ fer _ no a sue   pre _

_ ghie _ re Glo _ ria immortal di Pin _ do   e   d'E _ li _ co _ _ na.

Ritornello

Hor mentre i canti al_ter_no hor lie_ti hor me_sti non si mo_va

Au_gel_lin fra que_ste pian_te ne s'o_da

in que_ste ri_ve on_da so_nan_te et o_gni au_

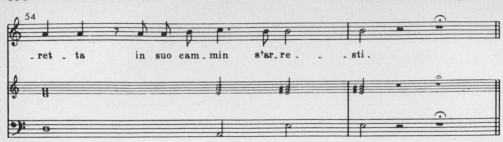

_ret _ ta   in suo cam _ min   s'ar _ re _   _ sti.

Ritornello
(Allegro)

b) *Act II, Orfeo,* Vi ricorda o boschi ombrosi *(excerpt)*

ORFEO

Vi ri_cor_da o bo_schi ombro _ si   Vi ri _cor_ da o boschi om_

(Più tranquillo)

_bro _ si de'miei lungh'aspri tor_menti quandoi sassi ai miei la_men_ti rispondean fat_ti pie_

_to _ si Vi ri_cor_da o bo_sch'om_bro _ si ,   vi ri_cor_ da o bo_sch'om bro_ si.

c) *Act II, Messagera*, In un fiorito prato
       Orfeo, Tu se' morta
      Choro, Ahi caso acerbo

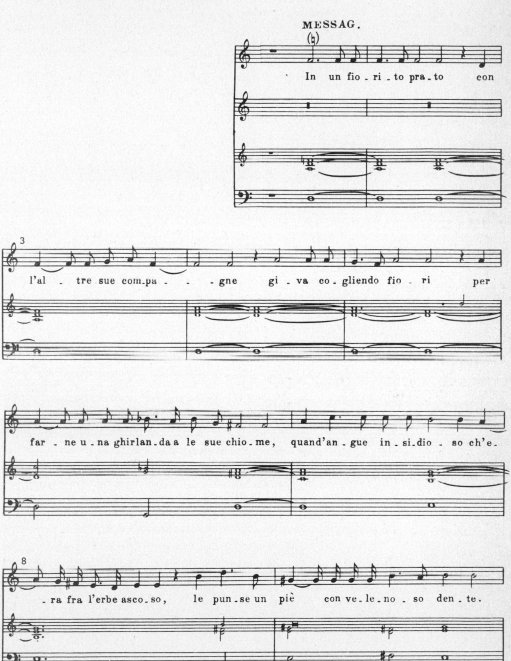

può do_ler_si; Ahi   ben havrebbeuncordi Tigre o d'Orsa   chi non sentis_se

40

del tuo mal   pie_ta_te,   pri_vo d'ogni tuo ben mi _ se_ro a_man _ te.

ORFEO

                         Tu   se' mor_ta   se' mor_ta mia vi_

Un organo di legno e un chitarone
(Largo)

46

_ta   ed io respi _ _ro,   tu   se' da me par_ti _ta,

se' da me par_ti _ ta per mai più,   mai più non torna_re ed io ri_man_

_go, no, no, che se i ver_si al_cu_na co _ sa pon _ no,

n'andrò si _ cu _ ro a più profon _ di a _ bis _ si   e in _ te _ ne _ ri _ to il

cor   del Re   de l'om_bre   me_co trar_rot _ ti   a ri_ve_der le

stel _ le,   O se ciò ne_ghe _ rammi em _ pio de_sti _ no,

ri_marrò te_co   in compagnia   di mor _ te   a dio ter _ ra

(Andante)

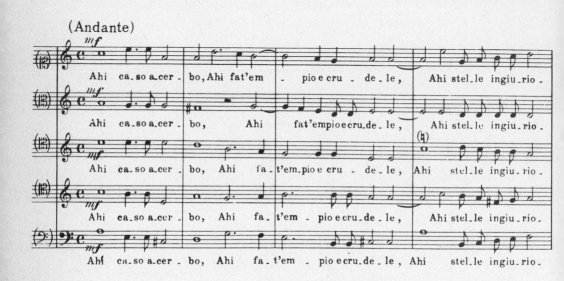

MUSIC

Dal mio Permesso amato a voi ne vegno,	From my beloved Permessus I come to you,
Incliti Eroi, sangue gentil de' Regi	Illustrious heroes, noble blood of kings,
Di cui narra la Fama eccelsi pregi,	of whom Fame relates their lofty worth,
Ne giunge al ver perch'è tropp'alto il segno.	yet falls short of the truth because the standard is too high.
Io la Musica son, ch'ai dolci accenti	I am Music, who, through sweet accents
So far tranquillo ogni turbato core,	know how to quiet every troubled heart,
Et hor di nobil' ira et hor d'amore	now with noble ire and now with love,
Poss' infiammar le più gelate menti.	I can inflame the most frozen spirits.

Io su cetera d'òr cantando soglio
Mortal orecchio lusingar tal'hora
E in questa guisa a l'armonia sonora
De la lira del ciel più l'alme invoglio.

Quinci a dirvi d'Orfeo desio mi sprona,

D'Orfeo che trasse al suo cantar le fere

E servo fè l'Inferno a sue preghiere
Gloria immortal di Pindo e d'Elicona.

Hor mentre i canti alterno hor lieti, hor mesti,
Non si mova augellin fra queste piante,
Ne s'oda in queste rive onda sonante,

Et ogni auretta in suo cammin s'arresti.

I, on kithara of gold am used to singing,
charming mortal ears on occasion,
and in this guise to the sonorous harmony
of the heavenly lyre, the spirits beguile.

Hence to tell you of Orpheus the desire spurs
me:
of Orpheus, who with his singing attracted the
beasts,
and made a servant of Hell with his pleas,
immortal glory of Pindus and Helicon.

Now while I alternate happy and sad songs,
not a bird moves among these trees,
nor is heard on these shores a resounding
wave,
and every little breeze arrests its course.

ORPHEUS

Vi ricorda, o boschi ombrosi,
de' miei lungh' aspri tormenti,
quando i sassi ai miei lamenti
rispondean, fatti pietosi?

Do you recall, o shady woods,
my long, bitter torments,
when the stones to my laments
replied, pitiable deeds?

MESSENGER

In un fiorito prato
Con l'altre sue compagne
Giva cogliendo fiori
Per farne una ghirlanda a le sue chiome,
Quand'angue insidioso,
Ch'era fra l'erbe ascoso,
Le punse un piè con velenoso dente:
Ed ecco immantinente
Scolorirsi il bel viso e nei suoi lumi
Sparir que lampi, ond'ella al sol fea scorno.
All'hor noi tutte sbigottite e meste
Le fummo intorno, richiamar tentando
Li spirti in lei smarriti
Con l'onda fresca e con possenti carmi;
Ma nulla valse, ahi lassa!
Ch'ella i languidi lumi alquanto aprendo,
E te chiamando Orfeo,
Dopo un grave sospiro
Spirò fra queste braccia, ed io rimasi
Piena il cor di pietade e di spavento.

In a flowered meadow
with her companions
she was going about gathering flowers
to make a garland for her hair,
when a treacherous serpent
that was hidden in the grass
bit her foot with venemous tooth:
Then at once
her face became pale, and in her eyes
those lamps that vied with the sun grew dim·
Then we all, frightened and sad,
gathered around calling, tempting
the spirits that were smothered in her
with fresh water and powerful songs.
But nothing helped, alas,
for she, opening her languid eyes slightly,
called to you, Orpheus,
and, after a deep sigh,
expired in these arms, and I remained
with heart full of pity and terror.

SHEPHERD

Ahi caso acerbo, ahi fat' empio e crudele!
Ahi stelle ingiuriose, ahi cielo avaro!

A l'amara novella
rassembra l'infelice un muto sasso,

che per troppo dolor non può dolersi.

Ah, bitter event, ah, wicked fate and cruel!
Ah, malicious stars, ah, greedy heavens!

The bitter news
has turned the unfortunate one into a mute
stone;
from too much pain, he can feel no pain.

Ahi ben havrebbe un cor di Tigre o d'Orsa
Chi non sentisse del tuo mal pietate,
Privo d'ogni tuo ben, misero amante!

Ah, he must have the heart of a tiger or a bear
who did not feel pity for your loss,
as you are bereft of your dear one, wretched
lover.

ORPHEUS

Tu se' morta, mia vita, ed io respiro?
Tu se' da me partita
Per mai più non tornare, ed io rimango?
No, che se i versi alcuna cosa ponno,
N'andrò sicuro a' più profondi abissi,
E intenerito il cor del Re de l'Ombre

You are dead, my life, and I still breathe?
You have departed from me,
never to return, and I remain?
No, for if verses have any power
I shall go safely to the most profound abyss,
and having softened the heart of the King of
the Shades

Meco trarrotti a riveder le stelle,

I shall bring you back to see the stars once
again,

O se ciò negherammi empio destino
Rimarrò teco in compagnia di morte,

and if this is denied me by wicked fate,
I shall remain with you in the company of
death.

A dio terra, a dio cielo, e sole, a Dio.

Farewell earth, farewell sky and sun, farewell.

CHORUS

Ahi caso acerbo, ahi fat'empio e crudele!
Ahi stelle ingiuriose, ahi cielo avaro!
Non si fidi huom mortale
Di ben caduco e frale
Che tosto fugge, e spesso
A gran salita il precipizio è presso.

Ah, bitter event, ah, wicked fate and cruel!
Ah, malicious stars, ah greedy heavens!
Trust not, mortal man,
in goods fleeting and frail,
for they easily slip away and after a great as-
cent the precipice is near.

ALESSANDRO STRIGGIO (1573–1630)

70   Claudio Monteverdi
L'Incoronazione di Poppea, Drama in Musica (*1642*): *Act I, Scene 3, Poppea and Nero*

Tutte le opere di Claudio Monteverdi, edited by G. Francesco Malipiero (Asolo, 1926; reprinted Vienna: Universal Edition), Vol. XIII, pp. 29–35. Used by permission of European American Music Distributors Corp. Sole U.S. Agent for Universal Edition, Vienna.

De _ _ i _ tà   nel co _ re.

POPPEA

Signor, deh non partire,   Sir, please don't go.
Sostien, che queste braccia   Allow these arms
Ti circondino il collo,   to encircle your neck,
Come le tue bellezze   as your beauty
Circondano il cor mio.   encircles my heart.

NERO

Poppea, lascia ch'io parta.   Poppea, let me go.

POPPEA

Nor partir, Signor, deh non partire   Don't leave, Sir, please don't go.
Appena spunta l'alba, et tu che sei   The dawn is barely breaking, and you, who
                                                                  are
L'incarnato mio Sole,   my incarnated Sun,
La mia palpabil luce,   my light made palpable,
E l'amoroso dì de la mia vita,   the loving day of my life,
Vuoi sì repente far da me partita!   want to part from me so quickly.

Deh non dir   Please, don't say
Di partir,   that you're leaving.
Che di voce sì amara a un solo accento   It is such a bitter word that from one hint of it,
Ahi, perir, ahi spirar quest'alma io sento.   ah, I feel my soul dying, expiring.

NERO

La nobiltà de nascimenti tuoi   The nobility of your birth
Non permette che Roma   does not permit that Rome
Sappia che siamo uniti.   should know that we are together,
In sin ch'Ottavia non riman' esclusa   until Ottavia is set aside,
Col repudio da me: Vanne, ben mio;   repudiated by me. Go, my dear.
In un sospir, che vien   within a sigh that rises
Dal profondo del cor   from the depths of my heart
Includo un bacio, o cara et un' a Dio,   I enclose a kiss, dearest, and a farewell.
Si rivedrem ben tosto, Idolo mio.   We shall see each other soon, my idol

POPPEA

Signor, sempre mi vedi,   My lord, you see me constantly;
Anzi mai non mi vedi.   rather, you never see me.
Perchè s'è ver, che nel tuo cor io sia   Because, if it's true that I am in your heart,
Entr' al tuo sen celata   hidden in your breast,
Non posso da' tuoi lumi esser mirata.   I cannot by your eyes be viewed.

NERO

Adorati miei rai,   My adored rays,
Deh restate homai   please stay, then;
Rimanti, o mia Poppea,   remain, O my Poppea,
Cor, vezzo, e luce mia.   my heart, my charm, my light.

POPPEA

Deh non dir. . . .   Please don't say . . .

NERO

Non temer, tu stai meco a tutte l'hore,   Do not fear; stay with me for all time,
Splendor negl'occhi, e deità nel core.   splendor of my eyes, goddess of my heart.

GIOVANNI FRANCESCO BUSENELLO
(1598–1659)

Pier Francesco Cavalli (*1602–76*)
Egisto: Lament of Climene, *Piangete occhi dolenti*

71

Flavio Testi, *La musica italiana nel seicento: il melodramma* (Milan: Bramante Editrice, 1970), pp. 300–01.

Piangete, occhi dolenti
E al flebil pianto mio
Pianga, la fonte e il rio.
Articolate accenti,
frondose e mute piante,
De' miei casi infelici,
Selvagge spettatrici
E narrate pietose
A chi di qua se n' passa l'empia mia sorte.
Ahi lassa! e l'altrui tradimento.
Al mesto mio lamento
E Progne e Filomela
Accompagnino i loro
Queruli e tristi canti.

GIOVANNI FAUSTINI (1619–51)

Weep, sorrowful eyes,
and to my mournful weeping
weep, spring and river.
Speak in articulate accents,
leafy and mute plants,
of my unhappy fate,
wild spectators,
and recount with pity
to those who come here my pitiless fate.
Alas, and the treachery of others.
To my sorrowful lament
Let Procne and Philomela
join their
querulous and mournful songs.

<table>
<tr><td>**72**</td><td>**Marc' Antonio Cesti** (*1623–69*)
Orontea (ca. *1649*): Act II, Scene 17,
Aria, *Intorno all'idol mio*</td></tr>
</table>

In —— tor – no all'i – dol mi – o, Spi – ra —— te —, pur —— spi – ra – te —

Edited by William Holmes (Wellesley: Wellesley Edition, No. 11, 1973), pp. 158–62.

me____, cor — te — si, cor — te — si au — ret ———— te_____.

Al mio ben__ che ri — po — sa Su l'a ———— li___ del ———— la

-la —— te-li per me __, lar ——————————— ve d'a — mo —— re _____.

Intorno all'idol mio	Around my idol
Spirate, pur spirate	breathe, just breathe,
Aure soavi e grate	breezes sweet and pleasant,
E nelle guance elette	and on the favored cheeks
Baciatelo per me, cortesi aurette.	kiss him for me, gentle breezes.
Al mio ben che riposa	To my darling, who sleeps
Su l'ali della quiete	on the wings of calm,
Grati sogni assistete,	happy dreams induce;
E'l mio racchiuso ardore	and my covert ardor
Svelateli per me, larve d'amore.	unveil to him, phantoms of love.

GIACINTO ANDREA CICOGNINI
(1606–before 1651)

73

Jean-Baptiste Lully (*1632–87*)
Armide, Tragédie en 5 actes et un
prologue (*1686*)

a) *Ouverture*

Edited by Robert Eitner, *Publikationen älterer praktischer und theoretischer Musikwerke,* Vol. XIV (Leipzig: Breitkopf &
Härtel, 1885), 1–3, 100–4.

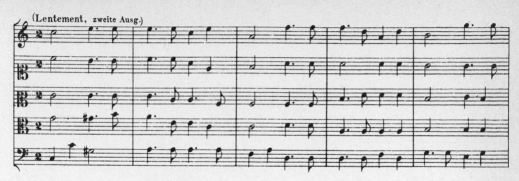

b) *Act II, Scene 5,* Enfin il est en ma puissance

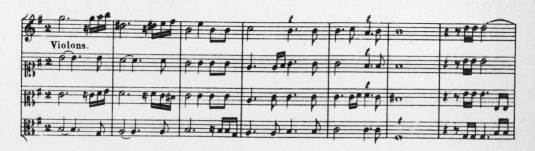

Armide. *(tenent un dard à la main.)*

En - fin   il est en ma puis-san-ce.   Ce fa-tal en-ne - mi,   ce su-per-be vain-

queur.   La char-me du som - meil-le liv-re à ma ven-gean-ce;   je vais per-cer son in-vin-ci - ble

(*Armide*

coeur.   Par lui tous mes cap-tifs sont sor-tis d'es-cla - va-ge; qu'il é-prou-ve tou-te ma ra - ge.   Quel

va pour frapper Renaud et ne peut exécuter le dessein qu'elle a de lui ôter la vie.)

trou-ble me sai-sit?   qui me fait hé - si - ter?   qu'est-ce qu'en sa fa - veur la pi-tié me veut

di - re? Frap-pons   ciel!   qui peut m'ar-ré - ter?   A-che vons...   je fré -

mis!   ven-geons-nous... je sou - pi - re!   Est-ce ain-si que je dois me ven-ger au-jour -

d'hui! Ma co-lè-re s'é - teint quand j'ap-pro-che de lui.   Plus je le   voi, plus ma ven-geance est

vai - ne; mon bras trem-blant se re-fuse á ma hai - ne. Ah!___ quel - le cru-au-

té de lui ra-vir le jour! A ce jeu-ne hé - ros tout cè - de sur la ter - re. Qui croi-

rait qu'il fut ne seu-le-ment pour la guer - re? Il sem - ble e-tre fait pour l'a - mour.

Ne puis - je me ven - ger à moins qu'il ne pé - ris - se? Hé! ne suf-fit il

pas que l'a-mour le pu - nis - se? Puis-qu'il n'a pu trou - ver mes yeux as-sez char-

mants, qu'il m'aime au moins par mes en - chan - te - ments, que s'il se peut, je le ha-

ïs - se.

Ve-nez, ve-nez, se-con-der mes dé-sirs, dé-mons, trans-for-mez vous en d'ai-ma-bles zé-phirs; ve-nez, ve-phirs. Je cède a ce vain-queur la pi-tié me sur-mon-te, ca-chez ma foi-

ARMIDE

Enfin il est en ma puissance,
Ce fatal ennemi ce superbe vainqueur.
Le charme du sommeille livre à ma vengeance;
Je vais percer son invincible cœur.
Par lui tous mes captifs sont sortis d'esclavage;
Qu'il éprouve toute ma rage.
Quel trouble me saisit? qui me fait hésiter?
Qu'est-ce qu'en sa faveur le pitié me veut dire?
Frappons . . . Ciel! qui peut m'arrêter?
Achevons . . . je frémis! vengeons—nous . . . je soupire!
Est-ce ainsi que je dois me venger aujourd'hui?
Ma colère s'éteint quand j'approche de lui.
Plus je le voi, plus ma vengeance est vaine;

Mon bras tremblant se refuse à ma haine.
Ah! quelle cruauté de lui ravir le jour!

Finally he is in my power,
this fatal enemy, this superb warrior.
The charm of sleep delivers him to my vengeance;
I will pierce his invincible heart.
Through him all my captives have escaped from slavery.
Let him feel all my anger.
What fear grips me? what makes me hesitate?
What in his favor does pity want to tell me?
Let us strike . . . Heavens! Who can stop me?
Let us get on with it . . . I tremble! Let us avenge . . . I sigh!
Is it thus that I must avenge myself today?
My rage is extinguished when I approach him.
The more I see of him, the more my vengeance is ineffectual.
My trembling arm denies my hate.
Ah! What cruelty, to rob him of the light of day!

A ce jeune héros tout cède sur la terre.

Qui croirait qu'il fut ne seulement pour la guerre?
Il semble être fait pour l'Amour.
Ne puis – je me venger à moins qu'il ne périsse?
Hé! ne suffit-il pas que l'amour le punisse?

Puisqu'il n'a pu trouver mes yeux assez charmants,
Qu'il m'aime au moins par mes enchantements,
Que, s'il se peut, je le haïsse.
Venez, venez, seconder mes désirs,
Démons, transformez – vous en d'aimables zéphirs.
Je cède à ce vainqueur, la pitié me surmonte.

Cachez ma foiblesse et ma honte
Dans les plus reculés déserts.
Volez, volez, conduisez – nous au bout de l'univers.

PHILIPPE QUINAULT (1635–88)

To this young hero everything on earth surrenders.

Who would believe that he was born only for war?
He seems to be made for love.
Could I not avenge myself unless he dies?

Oh, is it not enough that Love should punish him?
Since he could not find my eyes charming enough,
let him love me at least through my sorcery,

so that, if it's possible, I may hate him.
Come, come support my desires,
demons; transform yourselves into friendly zephyrs.
I give in to this conqueror; pity overwhelms me.
Conceal my weakness and my shame
in the most remote desert.
Fly, fly, lead us to the end of the universe.

74

Henry Purcell (1659–95)
The Fairy Queen, An Opera in Five Acts (1692)

a) Thus the ever grateful spring

Text by Elkanah Settle (?) from Shakespeare's *Midsummer Night's Dream*. Reprinted by Broude Bros. (New York, 19--), pp. 134–36, 150–56, 179–82.

Spring, Does her yearly tri-bute bring, does her yearly tri - - - bute bring, does her yearly tri-bute

bring, does her yearly tri - - - bute bring, All your sweets before him lay, all your

sweets be-fore him lay, Then round his al-tar sing and play, All, all, all, all, all, all, all your

sweets before him lay, Then round his al-tar sing and play, then round _____

_____ his al-tar sing and play. Thus the ev-er grate-ful Spring, Does her yearly tri-bute

1st time *pp* 2nd *f*

bring, does her yearly tri - - - bute bring, does her year-ly tri-bute bring.

b) *The Plaint,* O let me weep

I shall ne-ver, shall ne-ver, shall ne-ver, shall never see him more.

7 6   4 3   4 3   #   #

c) Hark! The ech'ing air a triumph sings

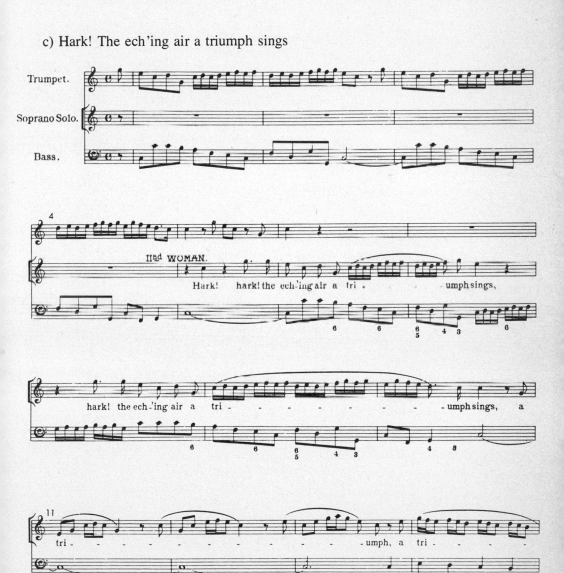

Trumpet.

Soprano Solo.

Bass.

IInd WOMAN.

Hark! hark! the ech'ing air a tri - umph sings,

6   6   6 5   4 3   0

hark! the ech'ing air a tri - umph sings, a

6   6   6 5   4 3   4 3

tri - umph, a tri - umph, a tri -

6   7 6   6

-round, and all a - round, pleas'd Cu - pids clap, clap,

clap, clap, clap their wings, clap, clap, clap, clap, clap, clap, clap their wings, pleas'd

Trumpet.

1st Violin.

2nd Violin.

Viola.

Cu-pids clap their wings And all a - wings.

CHORUS.
Soprano.

Hark! hark! hark! hark! hark!

Alto.

Hark! hark! hark! hark! hark!

Tenor.

Hark! hark! hark! hark! hark!

Bass.

Hark! hark! hark! hark! hark!

<table>
<tr><td>**75**</td><td>**Jean-Philippe Rameau** *(1683–1764)*
Hippolyte et Aricie, Tragédie en 5
Actes et un Prologue *(1733):* Act IV,
Scene 1, Aria, *Ah! faut-il*</td></tr>
</table>

Prélude

Tendrement

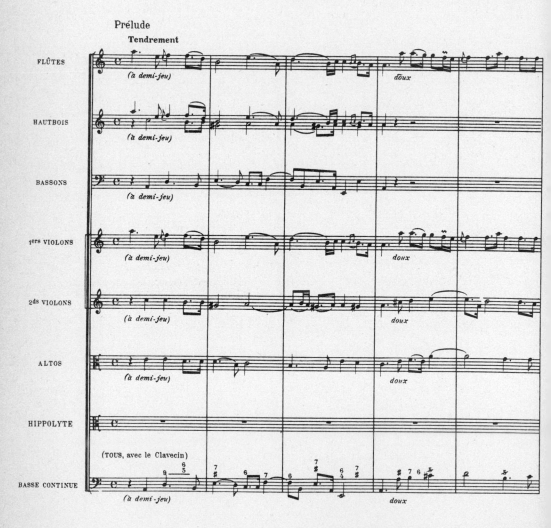

Rameau, *Oeuvres complètes,* VI, edited by Vincent d'Indy (Paris: Durand, 1900), pp. 262–67.

_me. Je ne ver_rai plus les beaux yeux Qui fai _ saient   mon bon_heur su_prê _ _ me.

Ah! faut-il, en un jour,   per _ dre tout cequej'ai _ me?

Ah! faut-il, en un jour, perdre tout ce que   Ah, must I, in a day, lose all that I love?
   j'aime?

Et les maux que je crains, et les biens que je   And the troubles I fear, and the riches I lose,
   perds,

Tout accable mon coeur d'une douleur ex-   all overwhelm my heart with extreme pain.
   trême.

Sous le nuage affreux dont mes jours sont cou-   Under the terrible cloud that darkens my days,
   verts,

Que deviendra ma gloire aux yeux de l'uni-   what will become of my glory in the eyes of
   vers?   the world?

Ah! faut-il, en un jour, perdre tout ce que   Ah, must I, in a day, lose all that I love?
   j'aime?

Mon père pour jamais me bannit de ces lieux   My father is banishing me forever from these
                                                parts

Si chéris de Diane même.   so dear to Diane herself.
Je ne verrai plus les beaux yeux   I shall see no more the beautiful eyes
Qui faisaient mon bonheur suprême.   which made me supremely happy.

     SIMON–JOSEPH PELLEGRIN (1663–1745)

Alessandro Scarlatti *(1660–1725)*
Griselda: Act II, Scene 1, Aria, *Mi rivedi, o selva ombrosa*

76

più Re - gi - na e spo - sa,   mi ri - ve - di sven - tu - ra - ta,   di-sprez-za-ta pa-sto-rel - la.

Mi ri - ve - di o sel - va om-bro - sa,   ma non più Re-gi - na e spo - sa,   mi ri-

ve - di sven-tu - ra - ta,   mi ri - ve-di sven - tu - ra - ta, di-sprez-za-ta, di-sprez-za-ta pa-sto-rel - la,   sven-tu

Dal segno

GRISELDA

Mi rivedi o selva ombrosa,
Ma non più Regina e sposa,
Sventurata, disprezzata
Pastorella.
È pur quello il patrio monte,
Questa è pur l'amica fonte,
Quello è il prato e questo è il rio;
E sol io non son più quella.

You see me again, o shady forest,
but no longer queen and bride;
unfortunate, disdained,
a shepherdess.
Yet there is my homeland's mountain
and here is still the friendly fountain;
there is the meadow and this is the river;
and only I am not the same.

Based on the libretto by
APOSTOLO ZENO (1668–1750)

Handel, *Werke*, edited by Friedrich Chrysander, Vol. 68 (Leipzig: Breitkopf und Härtel, 1875), pp. 102–8.

Dall' on-do - so pe - riglio   sal_vo mi por_ta al   li_do   il mio pro-pi_zio   fa_to.   Qui la ce_le_ste

par_ca   non tron_ca an _ cor   lo sta_me al _la mia   vi_ta!   Mà do_ve an _ drò?   e

chi mi por_ge a _ i _ ta?   o_ve son le mie schie_re?   o_ve   son le le_gio_ni,

che a tan_te mie vit _ to_ rie il var_co a   pri_ro!   So _ lo   in que-

CAESAR

Dall'ondoso periglio	From the perilous sea
Salvo mi porta al lido	safely takes me to the beach,
Il mio propizio fato.	my propitious destiny.
Quì la celeste parca	Here heavenly fate
Non tronca ancor lo stame a la mia vita!	does not yet cut the thread of my life.
Mà dove andrò e chi mi porge aita?	But where shall I go and who will come to my aid?
Ove son le mie schiere?	Where are my ranks?
Ove son le legioni,	Where are my legions,
Che a tante mie vittorie il varco apriro?	that to so many victories opened the way?
Solo in queste erme arene	In these solitary arenas
Al monarca del mondo errar conviene?	only the King of the World is at home.
Aure, aure, deh, per pietà	Breezes, for pity's sake,
Spirate al petto mio,	breathe on my breast
Per dar conforto, oh Dio!	to comfort me, O God,
Al mio dolor.	in my pain.
Dite, dite dov'è	Tell me, where is she,
Che fà l'idolo del mio sen,	where is the idol of my heart,
L'amato e dolce ben	beloved and sweet object
Di questo cor.	of this heart.
Mà d'ogni intorno i' veggio	But all around me I see,
Sparse d'arme e d'estinti	strewn with weapons and corpses,
L'infortuna arene,	this unfortunate arena,
Segno d'infausto annunzio al fin sarà.	an ill omen of my end.

NICOLA HAYM (1679–1729)

John Gay (1685–1732)*
The Beggar's Opera: Scenes 11 to 13.

78

Scene XI

MRS. PEACH

The thing, husband, must and shall be done. For the sake of intelligence we must take other measures, and have him peach'd the next Session without her consent. If she will not know her duty, we know ours.

PEACH

But really, my dear, it grieves one's heart to take off a great man. When I consider his personal bravery, his fine strategem, how much we have already got by him, and how much more we may get, methinks I can't find in my heart to have a hand in his death. I wish you could have made Polly undertake it.

MRS. PEACH

But in a case of necessity, our own lives are in danger.

PEACH

Then, indeed, we must comply with the customs of the world, and make gratitude give way to interest. He shall be taken off.

MRS. PEACH

I'll undertake to manage Polly.

PEACH

And I'll prepare matters for the Old–Baily.

Scene XII

POLLY

Now I'm a wretch, indeed. Methinks I see him already in the cart, sweeter and more lovely than the nosegay in his hand! I hear the crowd extolling his resolution and intrepidity! What vollies of sighs are sent from the windows of Holborn, that so comely a youth should be brought to disgrace! I see him at the tree! The whole Circle are in tears! Even Butchers weep! Jack Ketch himself hesitates to perform his duty, and would be glad to lose his fee, by a reprieve. What then will become of Polly! As yet I

*author of new texts set to existing songs. Gay's song texts are arranged in the left-hand column, the original texts and their sources in the right. Text and notes from *The Beggar's Opera by John Gay*, ed. Louis Kronenberger and Max Goberman (Larchmont: Argonaut Books, 1961), pp. xxxii–xxxiv.

may inform him of their design, and aid him in his escape. It shall be so. But then he flies, absents himself, and I bar myself from his dear dear conversation! That too will distract me. If he keep out of the way, my Papa and Mama may in time relent, and we may be happy. If he stays, stays, he is hang'd, and then he is lost for ever! He intended to lye conceal'd in my room, 'till the dusk of the evening: If they are abroad I'll this instant let him out, lest some accident should prevent him.

Exit, and returns

Scene XIII

Air XIV

MACHEATH

Pretty Polly, say	Pretty Parret say,
When I was away,	When I was away,
Did your fancy never stray	And in dull absence pass'd the Day;
To some newer lover?	What at home was doing;
Without disguise,	With Chat and Play,
Heaving sighs,	We are Gay,
Doating eyes,	Night and Day,
My constant heart discover.	Good Chear and Mirth Renewing;
Fondly let me loll!	Singing, Laughing all,
[Fondly let me loll!]	Singing, Laughing all,
O pretty, pretty Poll.	Like pretty, pretty Poll.

PILLS TO PURGE MELANCHOLY—Vol. V

POLLY

And are you as fond as ever, my dear?

MACHEATH

Suspect my honour, my courage, suspect anything but my love. May my pistols miss fire, and my mare flip her shoulder while I am pursu'd, if I ever forsake thee!

POLLY

Nay, my dear, I have no reason to doubt you, for I find in the Romance you lent me, none of the great Heroes were ever false in love.

Air XV

MACHEATH

My heart was so free,	Come Fair one be kind,
It rov'd like the Bee,	You never shall find,
'Till Polly my passon requited;	A Fellow so fit for a Lover;
I sipt each flower,	The World shall view,
I chang'd every hour,	My Passion for you,
[I sipt each flower,	The World shall view,
I chang'd every hour,]	My Passion for you,
But here ev'ry flower is united.	But never your Passion discover.

PILLS TO PURGE MELANCHOLY—Vol. IV

POLLY

Were you sentenc'd to Transportation, sure, my dear, you could not leave me behind you—could you?

MACHEATH

Is there any power, any force that could tear me from thee? You might sooner tear a pension out of the hands of a Courtier, a fee from a Lawyer, a pretty woman from a looking–glass, or any woman from Quadrille. But to tear me from thee is impossible!

Air XVI

Were I laid on Greenland's coast,	Jockey was a bonny Lad,
And in my arms embrac'd my lass;	And e'er was born in Scotland fair;
Warm amidst eternal frost,	But now poor Jockey is run mad,
Too soon the half year's night would pass.	For Jenny causes his Despair;
Were I sold on Indian soil,	Jockey was a Piper's Son,
Soon as the burning day was clos'd,	And fell in Love while he was young;
I could mock the sultry toil,	But all the Tunes that he could play,
When on my charmer's breast repos'd.	Was, o'er the Hills, and far away,
And I would love you all the day,	'Tis o'er the Hills, and far away,
Every night would kiss and play,	'Tis o'er the Hills, and far away,
If with me you'd fondly stray	'Tis o'er the Hills, and far away,
Over the hills and far away.	The wind has blown my Plad away.

PILLS TO PURGE MELANCHOLY—Vol. V

POLLY

Yes, I would go with thee. But oh! how shall I speak it? I must be torn from thee. We must part.

MACHEATH

How! Part!

POLLY

We must, we must. My Papa and Mama are set against thy life. They now, even now are in search after thee. They are preparing evidence against thee. Thy life depends upon a moment.

Air XVII

POLLY

O what pain it is to part!
Can I leave thee, can I leave thee?
O what pain it is to part!
Can thy Polly ever leave thee?
But lest death my love should thwart,
And bring thee to the fatal cart,
Thus I fear thee from my bleeding heart!
Fly hence, and let me leave thee.

Gin thou wer't my e'ne Thing,
I wou'd Love thee I wou'd Love thee.
Gin thou wer't my e'ne Thing,
So Early I wou'd Love thee.
I wou'd take thee in my Arms,
I'de Secure thee From all Harms,
Above all Mortals thou has Charms,
So Dearly do I love thee.

ORPHEUS CALEDONIUS

POLLY

One kiss and then—one kiss—begone—farewell.

MACHEATH

My hand, my heart, my dear, is so riveted to thine, that I cannot unloose my hold.

POLLY

But my Papa may intercept thee, and then I should lose the very glimmering of hope. A few weeks, perhaps, may reconcile us all. Shall thy Polly hear from thee?

MACHEATH

Must I then go?

POLLY

And will not absence change your love?

MACHEATH

If you doubt it, let me stay—and be hang'd.

POLLY

O how I fear! How I tremble! Go. But when safety will give you leave, you will be sure to see me gain; for 'till then Polly is wretched.

Air XVIII

fight 'tis gone, Whines, whimpers, sobs and cries.

The Miser thus a shilling sees,
Which he's oblig'd to pay,
With sighs resigns it by degrees,
And fears 'tis gone for aye.
The Boy thus, when his Sparrow's flown,
The bird in silence eyes;
But soon as out of sight 'tis gone,
Whines, whimpers, sobs and cries.

O ye Broom, ye bonny, bonny Broom,
The Broom of Cowden-knows,
I wish I were at Home again
To milk my Daddys Ews.
How blyth ilk Morn was I to see
The Swain come o'er the Hill.
He skipt ye Burn and flew to me,
I met him with good Will.

79 George Frideric Handel
Serse

a) *Act I, Scene 1, Recitativo accompagnato*, Frondi tenere; *Aria*, Ombra mai fù

Violino I
Violino II
Viola
SERSE
XERXES
Bassi
(Violoncello, Violone, Cembalo)

Fron - di te - ne - re, e bel - le del mio pla - ta - no a - ma - to, per

voi ri - splen - da il Fa - to. Tuo - ni, lam - pì, e pro - cel - le non v'ol-trag - gi - no

mai la ca - ra pa - ce nè giun - ga a pro - fa - nar - vi au - stro ra - pa - ce.

Reprinted by permission of Bärenreiter-Verlag, Kassel, Basel, Tours, London from: *Hallische Händel-Ausgabe*, edited by Rudolf Steglich (Kassel, 1958), pp. 9–11; 18–20.

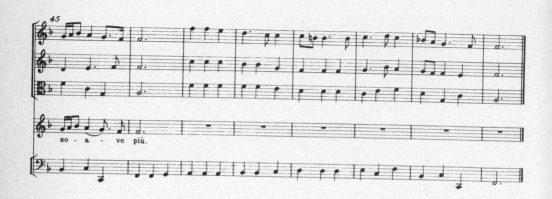

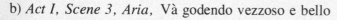

ma-bi- le, om - bra mai fù   di ve-ge-ta-bi-le   ca-ra ed a-ma-bi-le   so-a-ve più,

so - a - ve più.

b) *Act I, Scene 3, Aria*, Và godendo vezzoso e bello

Và go-den-do vez-zo-so e bel-lo quel ru-scel-lo la li-ber- tà.

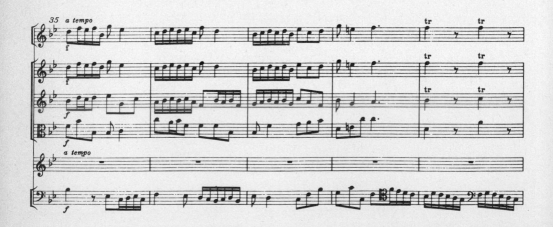

Frondi tenere, e belle
Del mio platano amato,
Per voi risplenda il Fato.
Tuoni, lampi, e procelle
Non v'oltraggino mai la cara pace
Nè giunga a profanarvi astro rapace.

Ombra mai fù di vegetabile
Cara ed amabile
Soave più.

Và godendo vezzoso e bello
Quel ruscello la libertà.
E tra l'erbe con onde chiare
Lieto al mare correndo và.

Based on the libretto by SILVIO
STAMPGILIA (1664–1725), which was
modeled on that by NICOLÒ MINATO (1654).

SERSE

Leaves, soft and lovely,
of my beloved plane-tree,
for you is Fate resplendent.
Thunder, lightning, and gales
never disturb your sweet peace;
nor are you reached by the curse of an angry
    star.

Never was there the shadow of a plant
more dear and lovable,
more sweet.

ROMILDA

Happily flowing, graceful and pretty,
the brook enjoys its liberty.
And among the grasses in clear ripples,
merrily it goes running to the sea.

<table>
<tr><td>80</td><td>**Giovanni Gabrieli** (*1554-7–1612*)
Motet: *Hodie completi sunt dies pentecostes* Antiphon at the Magnificat,
Second Vespers, Whitsunday</td></tr>
</table>

Gabrieli, *Symphoniae sacrae* (Venice, 1615). *Opera omnia*, edited by Denis Arnold, III (American Institute of Musicology) 1962), 44–56. Reprinted by permission of A. Carapetyan, Director and Hänssler-Verlag, West Germany. All rights reserved. International copyright secured. Reprinted by permission.

Hodie completi sunt dies pentecostes, alleluia: hodie Spiritus Sanctus in igne discipulis apparuit et tribuit eis charismatum dona: misit eos in universum mundum praedicare et testificari. Qui crediderit et baptizatus fuerit, salvus erit, alleluia.

Today are ended the days of Pentecost, alleluia. Today the Holy Ghost appeared in splendor to the disciples and bestowed upon them the gifts of grace. He sent them to preach and testify throughout the world. He who believed was both baptized and saved. Alleluia.

81

Lodovico Grossi da Viadana
(1560–1627)
Sacred concerto: *O Domine Jesu Christe*

Reprinted by permission of Bärenreiter-Verlag, Kassel, Basel, Tours, London, from: *Cento concerti ecclesiastici opera duodecima* (Venice, 1602), edited by Claudio Gallico (Kassel, etc., 1964), pp. 64–65.

O Domine Jesu Christe,
pastor bone,
justos`conserva
peccatores justifica,
omnibus fidelibus miserere,
et propitius esto mihi misero
et indigno peccatori. Amen.

O Lord Jesus Christ
good shepherd,
preserve the righteous,
do justice to the sinners,
have mercy on all the faithful,
and be gracious toward me, wretched
and unworthy sinner. Amen.

Values halved in triple meter. Compare this to the setting by Schütz of an almost identical text, page 448. *Ghirlanda sacra, Libro primo . . . per Leonardo Simonetti* (Venice, 1625). Edited by Rudolf Werhart in *Drei Hohelied Motetten,* Cantio sacra, no. 23 (Cologne: Verlag Edmund Bieler, 1960), pp. 7–9. Reprinted by permission.

O quam tu pulchra es, amica mea,
quam pulchra es, columba mea,
o quam tu pulchra es, formosa mea.
Oculi tui columbarum,
capilli tui sicut greges caprarum
et dentes tui sicut greges tonsarum.

O quam tu pulchra es.
Veni de Libano, amica mea,
columba mea, formosa mea.
O quam tu pulchra es,
veni, coronaberis.
Surge, surge, propera, sponsa mea,
surge,dilecta mea,
surge, immaculata mea.
Quia amore langueo.
Surge, veni, quia amore langueo.

SONG OF SONGS, 4:1, 4:8

Oh, how fair you are, my love,
how fair you are, my dove,
how fair you are, my beauty.
Your eyes, the eyes of doves,
your hair, like a flock of goats,
and your teeth like a flock of sheep newly
    shorn.
O how fair you are.
Come with me from Lebanon, my love,
my dove, my beauty.
Oh, how fair you are,
come, you will make a garland.
Arise, hasten, my bride,
arise, my delight,
arise, my spotless one.
For I pine of love. Arise,
come, for I pine of love.

83 Giacomo Carissimi *(1605–74)*
Historia di Jephte

a) *Filia,* Plorate, plorate colles

Edited by Gottfried Wolters, figured bass realized by Mathias Siedel (Wolfenbüttel: Möseler Verlag, 1969), pp. 29–39.
Reprinted by permission.

me do-len-tem in lae-ti-ti-a po-pu-li, in vi-cto-ri-a

Is-ra-el et glo-ri-a pa-tris me-i, e - go si-ne

fi-li-is vir - go, e-go fi-li-a u-ni-ge-ni-ta

mo-ri-ar et non vi -

vam. Ex-hor-re-sci-te ru-pes, ob-stu-pe-sci-te col-les,

ra - te fi - li - i Is - ra-el, plo - ra - te vir - gi-ni-ta-tem

me - am et Jeph - te fi - li-am u - ni - ge - ni-tam in car - mi-ne do-

lo - ris la - men-ta - - mi - ni, et

Jeph - te fi - li-am u - ni - ge - ni-tam in car - mi - ne do-

lo - ris la - men-ta - - mi - ni.

b) *Chorus,* Plorate filii Israel

Plorate colles, dolete montes
et in afflictione cordis mei
ululate! Ecce moriar virgo
et non potero morte mea meis
filiis consolari, ingemiscite
silvae, fontes et flumina, in interitu virginis lachrimate,
fontes et flumina.

Heu me dolentem in laetitia
populi, in victoria Israel
et gloria patris mei, ego
sine filiis virgo, ego
filia unigenita moriar et
non vivam. Exhorrescite
rupes, obstupescite colles,
valles et cavernae in sonitu
horribili resonate!
Plorate, filii Israel,
plorate virginitatem meam et
Jephte filiam unigenitam in
carmine doloris lamentamini.

Plorate filii Israel, plorate
omnes virgines et filiam Jephte
unigenitam in carmine doloris
lamentamini.

DAUGHTER

Weep, hills, grieve, mountains
and in the affliction of my heart,
wail! Suddenly I shall die a
virgin and I shall not be able at my death
to be consoled by my children. Groan,
forests, springs, and rivers. Weep
for the death of a virgin,
springs and rivers.

Woe is me, sorrowful, amidst the joy
of the people in the victory of Israel
and the glory of my country, I,
without children, a virgin; I,
an only daughter, will die and
not live. Shudder,
crags; be stupefied, hills;
valleys and caves, resonate
the horrible sound.
Weep, sons of Israel,
bewail my virginity and lament
Jephte's only daughter in
songs of sorrow.

CHORUS

Weep, sons of Israel; weep,
all virgins, and lament Jephthe's
only daughter in songs of
sorrow.

84

Heinrich Schütz (1585–1672)
Motet: *O quam tu pulchra es*

Compare to the setting by Grandi of almost the same text, p. 432. *Symphoniae sacrae* I (Venice, 1629). Reprinted by permission of Bärenreiter-Verlag, Kassel, Basel, Tours, London from: *Neue Ausgabe sämtlicher Werke,* Band 13, edited by Rudolf Gerber (Kassel, 1957), pp. 80–7.

O quam tu pulchra es, amica mea,
columba mea, formosa mea, immaculata mea.
O quam tu pulchra es.
Oculi tui columbarum.
Capilli tui sicut greges caprarum.
Dentos tui sicut greges tonsarum.
Sicut vita coccinea labia tua.
Sicut turris David collum.
Duo ubera tua sicut duo hinnuli
capre gemelli.

How fair you are, my love,
my dove, my beautiful, spotless love.
How fair you are.
Your eyes are like eyes of doves,
your hair, like a flock of goats,
your teeth like a flock of sheep newly shorn,
like a strand of scarlet, your lips,
like the tower of David, your neck,
your two breasts, like twin roes
born of a goat.

Pelham Humfrey (1647–74)
Verse Anthem: *Hear O heav'ns*

85

Humfrey, *Complete Church Music,* edited by Peter Dennison (Musica Britannica, Vol. 34–35) (London: Published for the Royal Musical Association, Stainer & Bell, 1972), pp. 82–89.

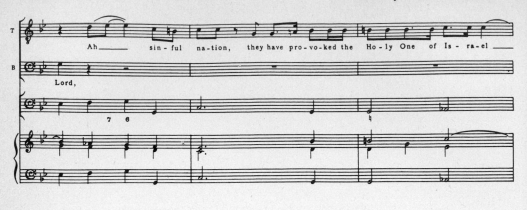

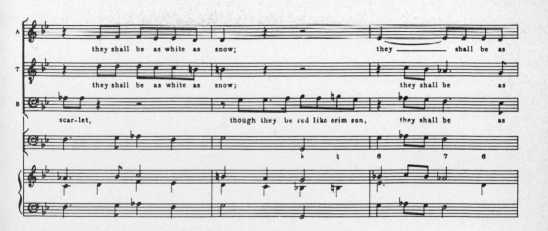

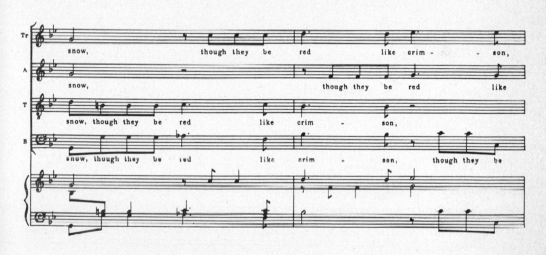

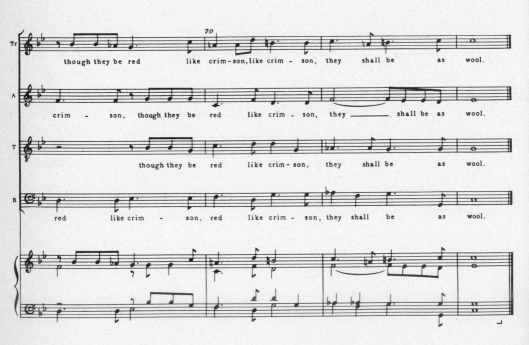

Francesco Antonio Urio (c1660–?)
Te Deum: Chorus, *Sanctum quoque paraclitum*

86

Händel, *Werke*, edited by Friedrich Chrysander, *Supplemente enthaltend Quellen zu Händel's Werken*, II (Leipzig, 1902), 64–67. By permission of Breitkopf & Härtel, Wiesbaden.

Sanctum quoque paraclitum spiritum   Also the Holy Ghost, the comforter.

George Frideric Handel
Saul, An Oratorio or Sacred Drama (*1739*): Act I, no. 4, Chorus, *The Youth inspir'd by Thee, O Lord*

87

Reprinted by permission of Bärenreiter-Verlag, Kassel, Basel, Tours, London from *Hallische Händel-Ausgabe*, Serie I, Band 13, edited by Percy M. Young. (Kassel, 1962), pp. 38–50.

Text by CHARLES JENNENS (1700–73)

88 Johann Sebastian Bach (1685–1750) Cantata, *Nun komm, der Heiden Heiland,* BWV 61 (*1714*)

1a) *Hymn,* Veni redemptor gentium

Ve - ni, re - dem - ptor gen - ti - um, o - sten - de par - tum vir - gi - nis;

mi - re - tur om - ne sae - cu - lum, ta - lis de - cet par - tus de - um.

Einsiedeln, Benediktinerkloster, Musikbibliothek, MS 366 (12th century), after Bruno Stäblein, ed., *Die mittelalterlichen Hymnenmelodien des Abendlandes, Monumenta monodica medii aevi,* Vol. I, Hymnen (I), pp. 273–74.

1b) *Chorale,* Nun komm, der Heiden Heiland,
Melody based on Hymn, Veni redemptor gentium

Nunn komm der Hei - den Hei - land, Der Jung - frau - en Kind er - kannt;

Dass sich wun - der al - le Welt. Gott solch Ge - burt ihm be - stellt.

Enchiridion Oder eyn Handbuchlein . . . geystlicher gesenge (Erfurt, 1524), after Johannes Zahn, *Die Melodien der deutschen evangelischen Kirchenlieder* (Gütersloh, 1892), Vol. I, No. 1174.

1c) *Chorus*, Nun komm, der Heiden Heiland

Music reprinted by permission of Bärenreiter-Verlag, Kassel, Basel, Tours, London from: *Neue Ausgabe sämtlicher Werke* Serie I, Band 1 edited by A. Dürr and W. Neumann. (Kassel, etc. 1954), pp. 3–16.

2) *Recitative,* Der Heiland ist gekommen

3) *Aria,* Komm, Jesu, komm zu deiner Kirche

Da Capo dal Segno 𝄋

4) *Recitative,* "Siehe, ich stehe vor der Tür"

5) *Aria,* Öffne dich, mein ganzes Herze

6a) *Chorale*, Wie schön leuchtet der Morgenstern
Melody by Philipp Nicolai

Wie schön leuch - tet der Mor - gen - stern. voll Gnad' und Wahr - heit von dem Herrn,
Du Sohn Da - vids aus Ja - kobs Stamm, mein Kö - nig und mein Bräu - ti - gam,

die füs - se Wur - zel Jes - se! lieb - lich, freund - lich, schön und herr - lich,
hast mir mein Herz be - ses - sen,

gross und ehr - lich, reich von Ga - ben, hoch und sehr präch - tig er - ha - ben.

Frewden Spiegel dess ewiger Lebens . . . durch Philippum Nicolai (Frankfurt, 1599), after Johannes Zahn, *Die Melodien der deutschen evangelischen Kirchenlieder* (Gütersloch, 1892), Vol. V, No. 8359.

6b) *Chorale*, Amen. Komm du schöne Freudenkrone.

Hymn

Veni, redemptor gentium,
ostende partum virginis;
miretur omne saeculum,
talis decet partus deum.

Come, Savior of nations,
display the offspring of the Virgin.
Let all ages marvel
that God granted such a birth.

Chorale

Nun komm der Heiden Heiland
Der Jungfrauen Kind erkannt,
Des sich wundert alle Welt,
Gott solch Geburt ihm bestellt.

Now come, gentiles' Savior,
child, known to be born of the Virgin,
at which all the world marveled
that God such a birth for him ordained.

Recitative

Der Heiland ist gekommen,
Hat unser armes Fleisch und Blut
An sich genommen
Und nimmet uns zu Blutsverwandten an.
O allerhöchstes Gut,
Was hast du nicht an uns getan?
Was tust du nicht
Noch täglich an den Deinen?
Du kömmst und lässt dein Licht
Mit vollem Segen scheinen.

The Savior has arrived;
He has our poor flesh and blood assumed,
and receives us as His blood-related kin.
O Supreme Good,
what have You not done for us?
What do You not
still daily do for Yours?
You come and leave Your light
with full blessings shining.

Aria

Komm, Jesu, komm zu deiner Kirche
Und gib ein selig neues Jahr!

Come, Jesus, come to your church,
and give a blessed new year!

Befördre deines Namens Ehre,
Erhalte die gesunde Lehre
Und segne Kanzel und Altar!

Advance Your name's honor,
preserve the sane doctrine,
and bless chancel and altar!

Recitative

"Siehe, ich stehe vor der Tür
und klopfe an. So jemand meine
Stimme hören wird und die Tür
auftun, zu dem werde ich eingehen
und das Abendmahl mit ihm halten
und er mit mir.''

"Behold, I stand at the door and
knock: if any man hear my
voice, and open the door,
I will come into him
and will sup with him,
and he with me.''

Aria

Öffne dich, mein ganzes Herze,
Jesus kömmt und ziehet ein.
Bin ich gleich nur Staub und Erde,
Will er mich doch nicht verschmähn,
Seine Lust an mir zu sehn,
Dass ich seine Wohnung werde.
O wie selig werd ich sein!

Open up, my whole heart,
Jesus comes and takes possession.
Though I am only dust and earth,
Still He will not disdain
to show His delight
that I become His dwelling place.
O how blessed will I be!

Chorale

Wie schön leuchtet der Morgenstern,
Voll Gnad und Wahrheit von dem Herrn,
Die füsse Wurzel Jesse!
Du Sohn Davids aus Jakobs Stamm,
Mein König und mein Bräutigam,
Hast mir mein Herz besessen,
Lieblich, freundlich,
Schön und herrlich, gross und ehrlich,

How fairly shines the morning star,
full of grace and truth of the Lord,
the roots of the stock of Jesse.
You, son of David from Jacob's tribe,
my king and my bridegroom,
you have taken possession of my heart,
loving, friendly,
handsome and magnificent, grand and honor-
able,

Reich von Gaben,
Hoch und sehr prächtig erhaben.

richly gifted,
tall and splendidly noble.

Chorale

Amen,
Amen.
Komm du schöne Freudenkrone, und bleib
nicht lange.
Deiner wart' ich mit Verlangen.

Amen,
Amen.
Come, you beautiful crown of joy; and tarry
not.
I wait for you with longing.

a) Et in Spiritum sanctum Dominum

The title "Mass in B minor" was added after the composer's time. It is questionable whether the compilation constitutes a Mass or whether it can be said to be in B minor. (a) *Et in Spiritum;* and (b) *Confiteor* date from 1747–49; (c) *et expecto* is based on the Chorus, "Jauchzet, ihr erfreuten Stimmen" (second movement) of Cantata BWV 120, *Gott, man lobet dich in der Stille,* for the inauguration of the new town-council (*Rathswechsel*) in 1728 or 1729. Reprinted by permission of Bärenreiter-Verlag Kassel, Basel, Tours, London from: *Neue Ausgabe sämtlicher Werke,* edited by Friedrich Smend. (Kassel, etc. 1954), pp. 190–215.

b) Confiteor

c) Et expecto resurrectionem

For a translation of the text see p. 14.

Giovanni Legrenzi (1626–90)
Trio Sonata, La Raspona

90

Sonate a due, e tre di Giovanni Legrenzi, Libro primo, Opera seconda (Venice, 1655). Reprinted by permission of Bärenreiter-Verlag, Kassel, Basel, Tours, London, from *Hortus Musicus*, No. 31, edited by Werner Danckert (Kassel, 1949), pp. 3–7.

525

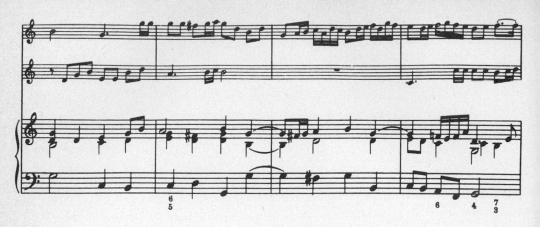

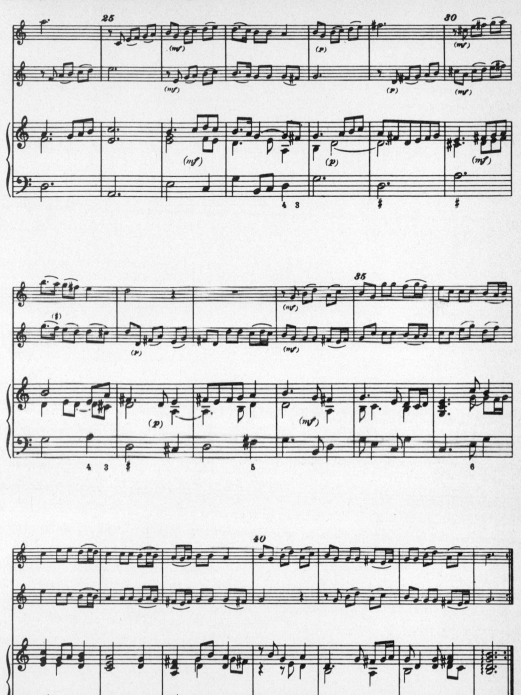

ADAGGIO

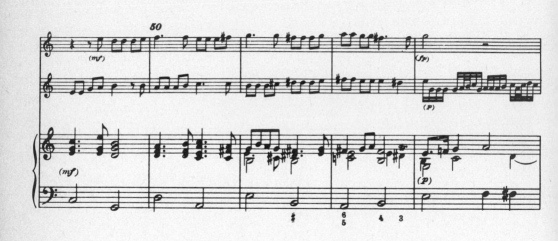

91

Arcangelo Corelli (1653–1713)
Trio Sonata, Opus 3, No. 2

Les Oeuvres de Arcangelo Corelli, edited by J. Joachim and F. Chrysander (London, n.d.), pp. 130–35.

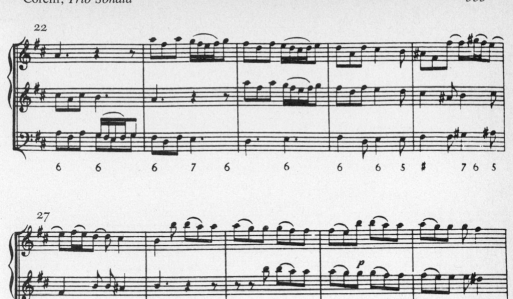

92 Antonio Vivaldi *(1678–1741)*
Concerto grosso in G Minor, Opus 3, No. 2

a) *Adagio e spiccato (first movement)*

Vivaldi, *L'Estro armonico,* Op. 3 (Amsterdam, 1712). Edited by Gian Francesco Malipiero (Milan: Ricordi, 1965), Vol. 407, pp. 1–33;F. IV, no. 8; Pincherle 326. Reprinted by permission.

b) *Allegro* (second movement)

20

30

35

75

(Solo)

Antonio Vivaldi
Concerto for Violin, Opus 9, No. 2:
Largo (second movement)

93

Vivaldi, *La Cetra* (Amsterdam, 1728). Edited by Gian Francesco Malipiero (Milan: Ricordi, 1952), Vol. 126, pp. 18–19; F. I, 51; Pincherle 214. Reprinted by permission.

Dietrich Buxtehudes Werke für Orgel, ed. Phillip Spitta, *Neue Ausgabe* von Max Seiffert, II (Leipzig, 1904), 1–2. Reprinted by permission of Breitkopf & Härtel, Wiesbaden.

Johann Sebastian Bach
Durch Adams Fall, BWV 637

a) *Chorale*

Durch A -dams Fall ist ganz ver-derbt Mensch - lich Na - tur und We - sen;
Das - selb Gift ist auf uns ge-erbt, Dass wir nicht moch-ten g'ne - sen

Ohn Got - tes Trost, der uns er - löst Hat von dem gros-sen Scha - den

Dar - ein die Schlang' Hie-nam be-zwang, Gotts Zorn auf sich zu la - den.

a) Text by Lazarus Spengler. *Geistliche Lieder auffs new gebossert* (Wittemberg: Joseph King, 1535), after Johannes Zahn, *Die Melodien der deutschen evangelischen Kirchenlieder* (Gütersloh, 1892), Vol. IV, No. 7549.

Durch Adams Fall ist ganz verderbt
Menschlich Natur und Wesen;
Dasselb Gift ist auf uns geerbt,
Dass wir nicht mochten g'nesen
Ohn Gottes Trost,
Der uns erlöst
Hat von dem grossen Schaden,
Darein die Schlang
Hienam bezwang,
Gotts Zorn auf sich zu laden.

LAZARUS SPENGLER

Through Adam's fall is entirely spoiled
both human nature and character.
The same venom was by us inherited,
so that we could not recover from it
without God's solace,
that saves us
from great harm;
for the serpent
somehow managed
to take onto itself God's anger.

b) *Organ chorale*

This is one of the chorales Bach entered into the *Orgel—Büchlein* (Little Organ Book), which he began to compile in Weimer (1716–17) and continued in Köthen (1717–23) but never finished.

<table>
<tr><td>

96

</td><td>

Johann Sebastian Bach
Chorale Preludes, *Wenn wir in höchsten Noten sein* (two settings)

</td></tr>
</table>

a) *Chorale tune*

| Wenn | wir | in | höch | | | sten | Nö | ten | sein | und | wis | sen | nicht, | wo | aus | noch | ein, |
| so | ist | dies | un | | | ser | Trost | al | lein, | daß | wir | zu | sam | men | ins | ge | mein |

| und | fin | den | we | der | Hilf | noch | Rat, | ob | wir | gleich | sor | gen | früh | und | spat, |
| dich | an | ru | fen, | o | treu | er | Gott, | um | Ret | tung | aus | der | Angst | und | Not. |

The text, by Paul Eber (1511–69), was set to this melody by Franz Eler in *Cantica sacra* (Hamburg, 1588). The melody was composed by Louis Bourgeois (*ca.* 1515–after 1561) to the French hymn, "Leve le coeur, ouvre l'oreille," published in *Psaulmes cinquante de David . . . traduictz en vers françois par Clément Marot* (Lyons, 1547).

Wenn wir in höchsten Nöten sein	When we are in greatest need
Und wissen nicht, wo aus noch ein,	and know not which way to go,
Und finden weder Hilf noch Rat,	and find neither help nor counsel,
Ob wir gleich sorgen früh und spat,	whether our worries come early or late,
So ist dies unser Trost allein,	then this alone is our comfort,
Dass wir zusammen insgemein,	that we together as one
Dich anrufen, o treuer Gott,	call upon you, o true God,
Um Rettung aus der Angst und Not.	for rescue from our anguish and misery.

b) *Organ Chorale, BWV 641*

From the *Orgel-Buchlein* (see No. 95). Reprinted by permission of Bärenreiter-Verlag, Kassel, Basel, Tours, London from *Neue Ausgabe sämtliche Werke*, Serie IV, Orgel Werke, Band 2, edited by Hans Klotz (Kassel, 1972), pp. 212-14.

c) *Organ Chorale, BWV 668a*

Edited by Hans Klotz from a Leipzig-period dictated copy (1750?) in *Neue Ausgabe sämtlicher Werke*, Serie IV, *Orgelwerke*, Band 2, pp. 212–14 (Kassel: Bärenreiter-Verlag, 1958); see the facsimile in *ibid.*, p. xiii. Reprinted by permission.

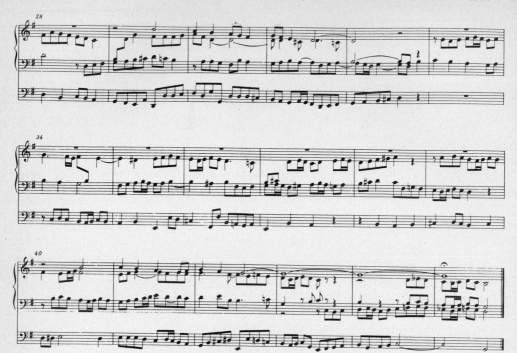

Johann Sebastian Bach
Praeludium et Fuga, BWV 543

97

Reprinted by permission of Bärenreiter-Verlag Kassel, Basel, Tours, London from: *Neue Ausgabe sämtliche Werke*, Serie IV, Orgel Werke, Band 5, edited by Dietrich Kilian (Kassel, 1972), pp. 186–97.

98 Variations on Dowland's *Lachrimae Pavan*

a) Dowland, *Lachrimae Pavan*

The Collected Lute Music of John Dowland, transcribed and edited by Diana Poulton and Basil Lam (London: Faber; Kassel: Bärenreiter-Verlag, 1974), pp. 67–70. Reprinted by permission.

b) William Byrd, *Pavana Lachrymae*

The Fitzwilliam Virginal Book, edited by J. A. Fuller Maitland and W. Barclay Squire (Leipzig: Breitkopf & Härtel, 1899), II, 42–46.

77

c) Giles Farnaby (ca. *1565–1640*), *Lachrimae Pavan*

d) Jan Pieterszoon Sweelinck (*1562–1621*), *Pavana Lachrimae*

Sweelinck, *Opera omnia*, Volume I, Fascicle III: Keyboard Works, Works for Lute, edited by Frits Noske (Amsterdam: copyright by Gustav Leonhardt, Alfons Annegarn and Frits Noske, 1968), pp. 42–46. Used by permission of Vereniging voor Nederlandse Muziekgeschiedenis.

Jan Pieterszoon Sweelinck
Fantasia a 4

Opera omnia, Vol. I: *The Instrumental Works*, edited by Gustav Leonhardt, Alfons Annegarn, and Frits Noske (Amsterdam: Vereeniging voor Nederlandse Muziekgeschiedenis, 1968), pp. 26–34. Used by permission of Vereeniging voor Nederlandse Muziekgeschiedenis.

Toccate d'intavolatura di cimbalo et organo, partite di diverse arie e corrente, balletti, ciaccone, passaghagli di Girolamo Frescobaldi, Libro primo (Rome, 1637). Reprinted by permission of Bärenreiter-Verlag, Kassel, Basel, Tours, London from: *Orgel- und Klavierwerke* III, edited by Pierre Pidoux (Kassel, 1954), pp. 60–66.

Ennemond Gautier (ca. 1575–1651)
La Poste (Gigue) for Lute

101

a) *The Gautier work for lute*

Special signs: ⌐) *pincé* (mordent with lower auxiliary); (ᖺ *coulé* (upward double appoggiatura); ♪ , (ᖺ *port de voix* (appoggiatura starting on lower auxiliary) *Oeuvres du vieux Gautier*, edited by André Souris (Paris: Éditions du CNRS, 1966), Nos. 63, 85, pp. 83, 111.

b) *An anonymous arrangement for harpsichord*

102

François Couperin (1668–1773)
Vingt-cinquième ordre (1730)
(excerpts)

a) La Visionaire

Gravement et marque

For a guide to the realization of Couperin's ornaments, see *HWM*, 381. *Pièces de Clavecin, 4ième Livre*, edited by Kenneth Gilbert © 1970 Heugel et Cie. Reprinted by permission. Theodore Presser Company, sole Representative U.S.A.

b) La Misterieuse

Modérement

c) La Monflambert

Tendrement, sans lenteur

d) La Muse victorieuse

Audacieusement

e) Les ombres errantes

Languissamment

Instrumental Names and Abbreviations

The following tables set forth the English, Italian, German, and French names used for the various musical instruments in these scores, and their respective abbreviations.

WOODWINDS

English	Italian	German	French
Piccolo (Picc.)	Flauto piccolo (Fl. Picc.)	Kleine Flöte (Kl. Fl.)	Petite flûte
Flute (Fl.)	Flauto (Fl.); Flauto grande (Fl. gr.)	Grosse Flöte (Fl. gr.)	Flûte (Fl.)
Alto flute	Flauto contralto (fl.c-alto)	Altflöte	Flûte en sol
Oboe (Ob.)	Oboe (Ob.)	Hoboe (Hb.); Oboe (Ob.)	Hautbois (Hb.)
English horn (E. H.)	Corno inglese (C. or Cor. ingl., C.i.)	Englisches Horn	Cor anglais (C. A.)
Sopranino clarinet	Clarinetto piccolo (clar. picc.)		
Clarinet (C., Cl., Clt., Clar.)	Clarinetto (Cl. Clar.)	Klarinette (Kl.)	Clarinette (Cl.)
Bass clarinet (B. Cl.)	Clarinetto basso (Cl. b., Cl. basso, Clar. basso)	Bass Klarinette (Bkl.)	Clarinette basse (Cl. bs.)
Bassoon (Bsn., Bssn.)	Fagotto (Fag., Fg.)	Fagott (Fag., Fg.)	Basson (Bssn.)
Contrabassoon (C. Bsn.)	Contrafagotto (Cfg., C. Fag., Cont. F.)	Kontrafagott (Kfg.)	Contrebasson (C. bssn.)

BRASS

English	Italian	German	French
French horn (Hr., Hn.)	Corno (Cor., C.)	Horn (Hr.) [pl. Hörner (Hrn.)]	Cor; Cor à pistons
Trumpet (Tpt., Trpt., Trp., Tr.)	Tromba (Tr.)	Trompete (Tr., Trp.)	Trompette (Tr.)
Trumpet in D	Tromba piccola (Tr. picc.)		

English	Italian	German	French
Cornet	Cornetta	Kornett	Cornet à pistons (C. à p., Pist.)
Trombone (Tr., Tbe., Trb., Trm., Trbe.)	Trombone [pl. Tromboni (Tbni., Trni.)]	Posaune.(Ps., Pos.)	Trombone (Tr.)
Tuba (Tb.)	Tuba (Tb, Tbaᵢ)	Tuba (Tb.)	Tuba (Tb.)

PERCUSSION

English	Italian	German	French
Percussion (Perc.)	Percussione	Schlagzeug (Schlag.)	Batterie (Batt.)
Kettledrums (K. D.)	Timpani (Timp., Tp.)	Pauken (Pk.)	Timbales (Timb.)
Snare drum (S. D.)	Tamburo piccolo (Tamb. picc.) Tamburo militare (Tamb. milit.)	Kleine Trommel (Kl. Tr.)	Caisse claire (C. cl.), Caisse roulante Tambour militaire (Tamb. milit.)
Bass drum (B. drum)	Gran cassa (Gr. Cassa, Gr. C., G. C.)	Grosse Trommel (Gr. Tr.)	Grosse caisse (Gr. c.)
Cymbals (Cym., Cymb.)	Piatti (P., Ptti., Piat.)	Becken (Beck.)	Cymbales (Cym.)
Tam-Tam (Tam-T.)			
Tambourine (Tamb.)	Tamburino (Tamb.)	Schellentrommel, Tamburin	Tambour de Basque (T. de B., Tamb. de Basque)
Triangle (Trgl., Tri.)	Triangolo (Trgl.)	Triangel	Triangle (Triang.)
Glockenspiel (Glocken.)	Campanelli (Cmp.)	Glockenspiel	Carillon
Bells (Chimes)	Campane (Cmp.)	Glocken	Cloches
Antique Cymbals	Crotali Piatti antichi	Antiken Zimbeln	Cymbales antiques
Sleigh Bells	Sonagli (Son.)	Schellen	Grelots
Xylophone (Xyl.)	Xilofono	Xylophon	Xylophone

STRINGS

English	*Italian*	*German*	*French*
Violin (V., Vl., Vln, Vi.)	Violino (V., Vl., Vln.)	Violine (V., Vl., Vln.) Geige (Gg.)	Violon (V., Vl., Vln.)
Viola (Va., Vl., *pl.* Vas.)	Viola (Va., Vla.) *pl.* Viole (Vle.)	Bratsche (Br.)	Alto (A.)
Violoncello, Cello (Vcl., Vc.)	Violoncello (Vc., Vlc., Vcllo.)	Violoncell (Vc., Vlc.)	Violoncelle (Vc.)
Double bass (D. Bs.)	Contrabasso (Cb., C. B.) *pl.* Contrabassi or Bassi (C. Bassi, Bi.)	Kontrabass (Kb.)	Contrebasse (C. B.)

OTHER INSTRUMENTS

English	*Italian*	*German*	*French*
Harp (Hp., Hrp.)	Arpa (A., Arp.)	Harfe (Hrf.)	Harpe (Hp.)
Piano	Pianoforte (P.-f., Pft.)	Klavier	Piano
Celesta (Cel.)			
Harpsichord	Cembalo	Cembalo	Clavecin
Harmonium (Harmon.)			
Organ (Org.)	Organo	Orgel	Orgue
Guitar		Gitarre (Git.)	
Mandoline (Mand.)			

Glossary

a. The phrases *a 2, a 3* (etc.) indicate that the part is to be played in unison by 2, 3 (etc.) players; when a simple number (1., 2., etc.) is placed over a part, it indicates that only the first (second, etc.) player in that group should play.

abdämpfen. To mute.

aber. But.

accelerando (acc.). Growing faster.

accompagnato (accomp.). In a continuo part, this indicates that the chord-playing instrument resumes (*cf. tasto solo*).

adagio. Slow, leisurely.

a demi-jeu. Half-organ; i.e., softer registration.

ad libitum (ad lib.). An indication giving the performer liberty to: (1) vary from strict tempo; (2) include or omit the part of some voice or instrument; (3) include a cadenza of his own invention.

agitato. Agitated, excited.

alla breve. A time signature (₵) indicating, in the sixteenth century, a single breve per two-beat measure; in later music, the half note rather than the quarter is the unit of beat.

allargando (allarg.). Growing broader.

alle, alles. All, every, each.

allegretto. A moderately fast tempo (between allegro and andante).

allegro. A rapid tempo (between allegretto and presto).

alto, altus (A.). The deeper of the two main divisions of women's (or boys') voices.

am Frosch. At the heel (of a bow).

am Griffbrett. Play near, or above, the fingerboard of a string instrument.

amoroso. Loving, amorous.

am Steg. On the bridge (of a string instrument).

ancora. Again.

andante. A moderately slow tempo (between adagio and allegretto).

animato,animé. Animated.

a piacere. The execution of the passage is left to the performer's discretion.

arco. Played with the bow.

arpeggiando, arpeggiato (arpeg.). Played in harp style, i.e. the notes of the chord played in quick succession rather than simultaneously.

assai. Very.

a tempo. At the (basic) tempo.

attacca. Begin what follows without pausing.

auf dem. On the (as in *auf dem G,* on the G string).

Auftritt. Scene.

Ausdruck. Expression.

ausdrucksvoll. With expression.

Auszug. Arrangement.

baguettes. Drumsticks (*baguettes de bois, baguettes timbales de bois,* wooden drumsticks or kettledrum sticks; *baguettes d'éponge,* sponge-headed drumsticks; *baguettes midures,* semi-hard drumsticks; *baguettes dures,* hard drumsticks; *baguettes timbales en feutre,* felt-headed kettledrum sticks).

bariton. Brass instrument.

bass, basso, bassus (B.). The lowest male voice.

Begleitung. Accompaniment.

belebt. Animated.

beruhigen. To calm, to quiet.

bewegt. Agitated.

bewegter. More agitated.

bien. Very.

breit. Broadly.

breiter. More broadly.

Bühne. Stage.

cadenza. An extended passage for solo instrument in free, improvisatory style.

calando. Diminishing in volume and speed.

cambiare. To change.

cantabile (cant.). In a singing style.

cantando. In a singing manner.

canto. Voice (as in *col canto,* a direction for the accompaniment to follow the solo part in tempo and expression).

cantus. An older designation for the highest part in a vocal work.

chiuso. Stopped, in horn playing.

col, colla, coll'. With the.

come prima, come sopra. As at first; as previously.

comme. Like, as.

comodo. Comfortable, easy.

con. With.

Continuo (Con.). A method of indicating an accompanying part by the bass notes only, together with figures designating the chords to be played above them. In general practice, the chords are played on a lute, harpsichord or organ, while, often, a viola da gamba or cello doubles the bass notes.

contratenor. In earlier music, the name given to the third voice part which was added to the basic two voice texture of discant and tenor, having the same range as the tenor which it frequently crosses.

corda. String; for example, *seconda (2a) corda* is the second string (the A string on the violin).

coro. Chorus.

coryphée. Leader of a ballet or chorus.

countertenor. Male alto, derived from *contratenor altus.*

crescendo (cresc.). Increasing in volume.

da capo (D.C.). Repeat from the beginning, usually up to the indication *Fine* (end).

daher. From there.

dal segno. Repeat from the sign.

Dämpfer (Dpf.). Mute.

decrescendo (decresc., decr.). Decreasing in volume.

delicato. Delicate, soft.

dessus. Treble.

détaché. With a broad, vigorous bow stroke, each note bowed singly.

deutlich. Distinctly.

diminuendo, diminuer (dim., dimin.). Decreasing in volume.

discantus. Improvised counterpoint to an existing melody.

divisés, divisi (div.). Divided; indicates that the instrumental group should be divided into two or more parts to play the passage in question.

dolce. Sweet and soft.

dolcemente. Sweetly.

dolcissimo (dolciss.). Very sweet.

Doppelgriff. Double stop.

doppelt. Twice.

doppio movimento. Twice as fast.

doux. Sweet.

drängend. Pressing on.

e. And.

Echoton. Like an echo.

éclatant. Sparkling, brilliant.

einleiten. To lead into.

Encore. Again.

en dehors. Emphasized.

en fusée. Dissolving in.

erschütterung. A violent shaking, deep emotion.

espressione intensa. Intense expression.

espressivo (espress., espr.). Expressive.

et. And

etwas. Somewhat, rather.

expressif (express.). Expressive.

falsetto. Male singing voice in which notes above the ordinary range are obtained artificially.

falsobordone. Four-part harmonization of psalm tones with mainly root-position chords.

fauxbourdon (faulx bourdon). Three-part harmony in which the chant melody in the treble is accompanied by two lower voices, one in parallel sixths, and the other improvised a fourth below the melody.

fermer bresquement. To close abruptly.

fine. End, close.

flatterzunge, flutter-tongue. A special tonguing technique for wind instruments, producing a rapid trill-like sound.

flüchtig. Fleeting, transient.

fois. Time (as in *premier fois,* first time).

forte (f). Loud.

fortissimo (ff). Very loud (*fff* indicates a still louder dynamic).

fortsetzend. Continuing.

forza. Force.

frei. Free.

fugato. A section of a composition fugally treated.

funebre. Funereal, mournful.

fuoco. Fire, spirit.

furioso. Furious.

ganz. Entirely, altogether.

gebrochen. Broken.

gedehnt. Held back.

gemächlich. Comfortable.

Generalpause (G.P.). Rest for the complete orchestra.

geschlagen. Struck.

geschwinder. More rapid, swift.

gesprochen. Spoken.

gesteigert. Intensified.

gestopft (chiuso). Stopped; for the notes of a horn obtained by placing the hand in the bell.

gestrichen (gestr.). Bowed.

gesungen. Sung.

geteilt (get.). Divided; indicates that the instrumental group should be divided into two parts to play the passage in question.

gewöhnlich (gew., gewöhnl.). Usual, customary.

giusto. Moderate.

gleichmässig. Equal, symmetrical.

gli altri. The others.

glissando (gliss.). Rapidly gliding over strings or keys, producing a scale run.

grande. Large, great.

grave. Slow, solemn; deep, low.

gravement. Gravely, solemnly.

grazioso. Graceful.

grossem. Large, big.

H⌐. *Hauptstimme,* the most important voice in the texture.

Halbe. Half.

Halt. Stop, hold.

harmonic (harm.). A flute-like sound produced on a string instrument by lightly. touching the string with the finger instead of pressing it down.

Hauptzeitmass. Original tempo.

heftiger. More passionate, violent.

hervortretend. Prominently.

Holz. Woodwinds.

hörbar. Audible.

immer. Always.

impetuoso. Impetuous, violent.

istesso tempo. The same tempo, as when the duration of the beat remains unaltered despite meter change.

klagend. Lamenting.

klangvoll. Sonorous, full-sounding.

klingen lassen. Allow to sound.

kräftig. Strong, forceful.

kurz. Short.

kurzer. Shorter.

laissez vibrer. Let vibrate; an indication to the player of a harp, cymbal, etc., that the sound must not be damped.

langsam. Slow.

langsamer. Slower.

largamente. Broadly.

larghetto. Slightly faster than largo.

largo. A very slow tempo.

lebhaft. Lively.

legato. Performed without any perceptible interruption between notes.

leggéro, leggiero (legg.). Light and graceful.

legno. The wood of the bow (*col legno tratto,* bowed with the wood; *col legno battuto,* tapped with the wood; *col legno gestrich,* played with the wood).

leidenschaftlich. Passionate, vehement.

lent. Slow.

lentamente. Slowly.

lento. A slow tempo (between andante and largo).

l.h. Abbreviation for "left hand."

lié. Tied.

ma. But.

maestoso. Majestic.

maggiore. Major key.

main. Hand (*droite,* right; *gauche,* left).

marcatissimo (marcatiss.). With very marked emphasis.

marcato (marc.). Marked, with emphasis.

marcia. March.

marqué. Marked, with emphasis.

mässig. Moderate.

mean. Middle part of a polyphonic composition.

meno. Less.

mezza voce. With half the voice power.

mezzo forte (mf). Moderately loud.

mezzo piano (mp). Moderately soft.

minore. In the minor mode.

minuetto. Minuet.

mit. With

M. M. Metronome; followed by an indication of the setting for the correct tempo.

moderato, modéré. At a moderate tempo.

molto. Very, much.

mosso. Rapid.

motetus. In medieval polyphonic music, a voice part above the tenor; generally, the first additional part to be composed.

moto. Motion.

muta, mutano. Change the tuning of the instrument as specified.

N⁻ . Nebenstimme, the second most important voice in the texture.

Nachslag. Auxiliary note (at end of trill).

nehmen (nimmt). To take.

neue. New.

nicht, non. Not.

noch. Still, yet.

octava (okt., 8va). Octave; if not otherwise qualified, means the notes marked should be played an octave higher than written.

ohne (o.). Without.

open. In brass instruments, the opposite of muted. In string instruments, refers to the unstopped string (i.e. sounding at its full length).

ordinario, ordinairement (ordin., ord.). In the usual way (generally cancelling an instruction to play using some special technique).

ôtez les sourdines. Remove the mutes.

parlando. A singing style with the voice approximating speech.

parte. Part (*colla parte,* the accompaniment is to follow the soloist in tempo).

passione. Passion.

pause. Rest.

pedal (ped., P.). In piano music, indicates that the damper pedal should be depressed; an asterisk indicates the point of release (brackets below the music are also used to indicate pedalling). On an organ, the pedals are a keyboard played with the feet.

perdendosi. Gradually dying away.

peu. Little, a little.

pianissimo (pp). Very soft (*ppp* indicates a still softer dynamic).

piano (p). Soft.

più. More.

pizzicato (pizz.). The string plucked with the finger.

plötzlich. Suddenly, immediately.

plus. More.

pochissimo (pochiss.). Very little.

poco. Little, a little.

poco a poco. Little by little.
ponticello (pont.). The bridge (of a string instrument).
portato. Performance manner between legato and staccato.
prenez. Take up.
près de la table. On the harp, the plucking of the strings near the soundboard.
prestissimo. Very fast.
presto. A very quick tempo (faster than allegro).
prima. First.
principale (pr.). Principal, solo.

quasi. Almost, as if.
quasi niente. Almost nothing, i.e. as softly as possible.
quintus. An older designation for the fifth part in a vocal work.

rallentando (rall., rallent.). Growing slower.
rasch. Quick.
recitative (recit.). A vocal style designed to imitate and emphasize the natural inflections of speech.
rinforzando (rinf.). Sudden accent on a single note or chord.
ritardando (rit., ritard.). Gradually slackening in speed.
ritmico. Rhythmical.
rubato. A certain elasticity and flexibility of tempo, speeding up and slowing down, according to the requirements of the music.
ruhig. Calm.
ruhiger. More calmly.

saltando (salt.). An indication to the string player to bounce the bow off the string by playing with short, quick bow-strokes.
sans. Without.
scherzando (scherz.). Playfully.
schleppend. Dragging.
schnell. Fast.
schneller. Faster.
schon. Already.
schwerer. Heavier, more difficult.
schwermütig. Dejected, sad.
sec., secco. Dry, simple.
segno. Sign in form of :S: indicating the beginning and end of a section to be repeated.
segue. (1) Continue to the next movement without pausing; (2) continue in the same manner.
sehr. Very.
semplice. Simple, in a simple manner.
sempre. Always, continually.
senza. Without.
senza mis[ura]. Free of regular meter.
serpent. Bass of the cornett family.
seulement. Only.
sforzando, sforzato (sfz, sf). With sudden emphasis.

simile. In a similar manner.
sino al . . . Up to the . . . (usually followed by a new tempo marking, or by a dotted line indicating a terminal point).
sombre. Dark, somber.
son. Sound.
sonore. Sonorous, with full tone.
sopra. Above; in piano music, used to indicate that one hand must pass above the other.
soprano (Sop., S.) The voice with the highest range.
sordino (sord.). Mute.
sostenendo, sostenuto (sost.). Sustained.
sotto voce. In an undertone, subdued, under the breath.
sourdine. Mute.
soutenu. Sustained.
spiccato. With a light bouncing motion of the bow.
spirito. Spirited, lively.
spiritoso. In a spirited manner.
sprechstimme (sprechst.). Speaking voice.
staccato (stacc.). Detached, separated, abruptly disconnected.
stentando, stentato (stent.). Delaying, retarding.
Stimme. Voice.
strepitoso, strepito. Noisy, boisterous.
stretto. In a non-fugal composition, indicates a concluding section at an increased speed.
stringendo (string.). Quickening.
subito (sub.). Suddenly, immediately.
sul. On the (as in *sul G,* on the G string).
suono. Sound, tone.
superius. The uppermost part.
sur. On.

Takt. Bar, beat.
tasto solo. In a continuo part, this indicates that only the string instrument plays; the chord-playing instrument is silent.
tempo primo (tempo I). At the original tempo.
tendrement. Tenderly.
tenerezza. Tenderness.
tenor, tenore (T., ten.). High male voice or part.
tenuto (ten.). Held, sustained.
touche. Fingerboard or fret (of a string instrument).
tranquillo. Quiet, calm.
trauernd. Mournfully.
treble. Soprano voice or range.
tremolo (trem). On string instruments, a quick reiteration of the same tone, produced by a rapid up-and-down movement of the bow; also a rapid alteration between two different notes.
très. Very.
trill (tr.). The rapid alternation of a given note with the note above it. In a drum part it indicates rapid alternating strokes with two drumsticks.
triplum. In medieval polyphonic music, a voice part above the tenor.
tristement. Sadly.
troppo. Too much.

tutti. Literally, "all"; usually means all the instruments in a given category as distinct from a solo part.

übertönend. Drowning out.

unison (*unis.*). The same notes or melody played by several instruments at the same pitch. Often used to emphasize that a phrase is not to be divided among several players.

Unterbrechung. Interruption, suspension.

veloce. Fast.

verhalten. Restrained, held back.

verklingen lassen. To let die away.

Verwandlung. Change of scene.

verzweiflungsvoll. Full of despair.

vibrato. Slight fluctuation of pitch around a sustained tone.

vif. Lively.

vigoroso. Vigorous, strong.

vivace. Quick, lively.

voce. Voice.

volti. Turn over (the page).

Vorhang auf. Curtain up.

Vorhang fällt, Vorhang zu. Curtain down.

voriges. Preceding.

vorwärts. Forward, onward.

weg. Away, beyond.

wieder. Again.

wie oben. As above, as before.

zart. Tenderly, delicately.

ziemlich. Suitable, fit.

zurückhaltend. Slackening in speed.

zurückkehrend zum. Return to, go back to.

Index of Composers

Index of Titles

Index of Forms and Genres

Index to NAWM references in Grout,
History of Western Music, 3rd ed.